D1015633

AROUND THE HOUSE AND IN THE GARDEN

A Memoir of Heartbreak, Healing, and Home Improvement

DOMINIQUE BROWNING

SCRIBNER

New York   London   Toronto   Sydney   Singapore

SCRIBNER
1230 Avenue of the Americans
New York, NY 10020

DESIGNED BY ERICH HOBBING

Text set in Granjon

Manufactured in the United States of America

1   3   5   7   9   10   8   6   4   2

Library of Congress Cataloging-in-Publication Data
Browning, Dominique.
Around the house and in the garden: a memoir of heartbreak, healing,
and home improvement / Dominique Browning.
p. cm.
1. Divorce—Psychological aspects. 2. Home—Psychological aspects.
3. Loss (Psychology) 4. Environmental psychology. 5. Home improvement.
6. Gardening—Therapeutic use. 7. Browning, Dominique.
8. Homemakers—United States—Biography. I. Title.
HQ814 .B78 2002
306.89—dc21
2001054958

ISBN 0-7432-2595-3

For information about special discounts for bulk purchases,
please contact Simon & Schuster Special Sales at
1-800-456-6798 or business@simonandschuster.com

Portions of this book have appeared, in altered form, in *House & Garden* magazine.

For Alex and Theo
and
for Nicole

CONTENTS

AROUND THE HOUSE
AND IN THE GARDEN

WHAT'S IT ALL ABOUT?

When I was divorced my sense of home fell apart. And so, too, did my house. The rooms looked ravaged, sacked as they were of furniture, art, books, the mementos of a life constructed with someone else; everything fallen into disrepair. For a long time I couldn't bring myself to buy new furniture. I couldn't replaster and repaint; it took too much energy even to consider choosing colors. Except for the children's rooms, I wanted everything to be clean, but empty, redolent of failed love. I was very, very sad. I went through days, months, and maybe even years fully able to be a good mother, and to be a friend, and to work—in fact, taking comfort in the time-consuming distraction of it as well as in the structure the job's demands gave to my days. It was only my house—disheveled, lonely-looking, pale, and crumbling—that showed the symptoms of my uneasiness in my new life.

I am a slowpoke, in some profound ways, and always have been. Some people bounce quickly out of divorce into new relationships, new marriages, and new houses; lucky for them, I say. But it took me years to renovate my attitude, and it was a messy job, proceeding in fits and starts. So there is no chronology in the writing that follows; there was no narrative to my heartbreak or my healing. Just a starting point— but maybe not even that, as divorce, or any kind of suffering, usually does not seem like the beginning of anything, just the end of something.

Strangely enough, my divorce came through when I was starting a new job as the editor of *House & Garden,* a magazine about making homes. Nothing in my professional background could have prepared me for this subject; I had worked at magazines like *Newsweek* and *Texas Monthly* and *Esquire,* which, if they have anything to do with home, say so only indirectly. Maybe because I was now making a living thinking about houses, I was more self-conscious about the state of my own home. But because I was so intensely busy with the magazine, I didn't have to press myself actually to do anything about it. I lived vicariously, in other people's tailored, well-appointed rooms, surrounded by their beautiful things. Whatever I was looking for I found in photographs that seemed always to capture domestic perfection. So long as the children were comfortable, I felt free to go my own, slow, meditative way in pulling things back together. My children saw that their house—one of their houses—looked strange, but they were graciously, instinctively generous in their acceptance of it.

I began to pay close attention to how people talk about making homes, whether they are decorators, architects, clients, or people like me, who have always done it—or not—themselves. I began to appreciate how deeply charged a subject home is; it really is not about chintz as opposed to toile—or it is that, and much more. We invest our homes with such hope, such dreams, such longing for love, security, a good life—and stylishness to boot. That's what I have been trying to explore in what follows. Sure, making a home is a materialistic endeavor. But it is often, maybe usually, undertaken with intense spiritual energy.

I cannot say my home healed my heart. But I can say that, as my heart healed, my home reflected it. Perhaps my house forced my hand, at times, with its unrelenting demands. And perhaps at times my heart, gladdened, let me turn my attention homeward. Whatever the strange, looping path I took out of sadness, it wound its way from room to room, like a recurring dream I had as a child, in which I kept looking for something in a cavernous, empty old house, never finding it, but never being able to stop the ceaseless searching, either.

Maybe my subject is yearning; maybe that's the case for most of us. We yearn to live in houses full of love, happiness, passion, and peace, too. We yearn for domestic bliss. Even when we have found it, we are restless about wanting things to be better. As soon as we get what we want, we want more. That's the nature of being alive, of persevering, of striving.

And that is the nature of redecorating.

WHEN IT WAS OVER

You always know when it's over, and it is almost never during one of those familiar moments of high drama— a big fight, a big betrayal, a big disgrace. We don't hit love's bottom with door-slamming, fist-clenching, sob-choking fury. That's when we're alive. Instead, the death of a relationship seems to creep up quietly, achingly; it makes its slow, sour presence felt in strange and subtle moments. The things you think you're fighting about—sex, money, work, children—those are never really the main event. They're the skewed translations of deeper problems, curled up in the dark belly of love: problems with fear, or grief, problems with scar tissue that may long ago have knit itself over too thickly.

When I think back over the unraveling of my marriage, things are clear now that were not then. But this story isn't about marriage, and in any event I intend to protect the privacy of a couple that no longer exists to protest the accuracy of anything I might say. My story begins with the end of a marriage, the end of a household, the end of a home. It is about mourning, and the passage through what I came to think of as a living death—or perhaps, living a death. And it is about the way a house can express loss, and then bereavement, and then, finally, the rebuilding of a life.

It was in the middle of one of our traditional Sunday lunch parties that I knew our marriage was permanently derailed. We were in our house in suburban New York; Nick and I had married young, for our East Coast circle, and we were the first to have children and live in a house. Because our friends were still living in their city apartments, we had to make special efforts to get them to ride the train, cross the river (a psychological deterrent for New Yorkers), and come for a visit "in the country"—as we billed it. The country: sidewalks, mailboxes, birds, trees, lawns, barbecue grills, sprinklers, swing sets, mowers, cars. A kitchen, full of bookcases and cupboards, that was not only roomy enough to cook a huge meal in but pleasant and comfortable to sit in as well (my own studio kitchen in New York City during my single days was shoehorned into a coat closet; I used the stove to heat the apartment).

Our house had a dining room, another novelty. Bedrooms for the children, their own playroom. And a guest room. We had it all, and our suburban life was so unusual that our friends came to see us with the slight hauteur and detached curiosity with which anthropologists would observe a new tribe. Little did they know that within a decade most of them would have their own houses and gardens and babies.

That late winter day, a fire was crackling in the fireplace next to the long table, and our guests, old friends and some new ones, were groaning with the pleasure of full bellies. Our faces were flushed with heat, wine, conversation. The moment that comes back to me began in the middle of some political argument, the gist of which I lost long ago.

I was drifting along with the conversation when I began to be overcome by a sensation of floating away, of disconnecting and hovering over the table. From somewhere outside of myself, I glanced around the beautiful dining room, admiring the golden quality of the late afternoon sun slanting in through windows whose glass was slumping into their panes under nearly a hundred years of age—all except one that had recently been shattered by a child's errant baseball. It caught my eye, its pristine flatness put into relief by the nearly liquid quality of the light. The trunks and bare branches of the trees outside seemed to be carved into the radiant sky.

The logs crackled and popped, the table danced—the striations of the wood looked alive. We had moved that table to New York from our first home together in Texas, where I had collaborated in designing it with a local cabinetmaker. Cooking was a passion of my husband's; eating was mine. I had a walloping china fetish, and loved to set a beautiful table, and to serve friends; I even loved to clean up. Dinner parties had become a kind of glue in the relationship that we had built over the last fifteen years; the table was a place where we could come together in a performance of partnership that gave us pleasure. I had grown up in a home where dinner parties were impossible. The anxiety of preparation was insupportable for my mother; my father, a surgeon, was liable to disappear to save a life and ruin a meal at any moment; it is doubtful that had we had guests at the table they could have withstood the sharp correction of their manners with every forkful—lessons my French mother inflicted on her children, that we not become boorish Americans. So it seemed something of a miracle to me that I had become a grown-up who could actually have friends at the table, and pots bubbling on the stove, and conversation about things we read in the paper—a miracle of tranquility, civility. An ideal.

That Sunday, everything gleamed with a patina of contentment, perfect domesticity.

Except that I seemed to be detaching from it all, peeling away. The sensation was so strong that I felt sure I must have a bubble over my head, filled with a life-size cartoon character, telling everyone—in fat, screaming capital letters— what I was really thinking. There I was, serving, passing, clearing, laughing, talking. There I was, smiling at my husband. And the bubble over my head said, What am I doing? You all think I'm here, and happy, and engaged, and I am not. And why am I not happy when everything is so beautiful, so polished? Why can't I engage with people I love, in a home I love? Why does it seem inconceivable to me, the idea of spending the rest of my life this way—this was so much a part of what I had wanted. Why can't this work?

I watched a candle sputter, and just as I became conscious that the flame was burning too far into the crystal candlestick, there was a slow, violent, cracking sound, and the hunk of gorgeous old glass split in two. The candlestick had been a wedding present from my father. The conversation was stilled by the geological drama of the moment. I stood to pick up the pieces, feeling myself move heavily with the weight of a sadness I had finally acknowledged. No one could see how charged a moment it was for me, and I'm not sure I understood it for a long time; I knew simply that the disturbance ran deep.

Nick and I blew out the rest of the candles later in the evening, when everyone had gone home. And as I had done dozens of times before, I put away silver and platters, threw linens into the washing machine, poked the logs apart in their iron cradle, picked wax drippings off the table and rubbed oil into its clean surface. I dimmed the lights in the dining room, gave it one last look, and closed the door.

That dining room stayed closed, and empty, for a long time.

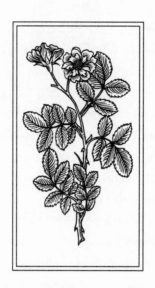

WHO GETS THE HOUSE?

The day eventually came—perhaps a year after that lunch party—when it was time for my ex-husband to move out of our house. A van was parked in the driveway, ramps were set up at the kitchen steps, burly men swept through the rooms, boxing things marked with a piece of red tape—his. The boys, who were five and nine years old at the time, had been packed off to my parents' house so they wouldn't have to witness the dismantling of their home. And then it was done.

As he was leaving, Nick took one last walk through a house that seemed awkward in its nakedness. He stopped in the kitchen and turned to me. "This was a paradise," he said. "I never knew you felt that way," I replied.

In the fifteen years we lived together, he had seemed oblivious to anything having to do with furnishing, decoration, arrangement. I had enjoyed setting up the household, shopping for it, and tending to each room's needs for chairs, rugs, lamps, art. I saw husbanding the home as one of my roles in the marriage, a way that I could show love, and nurture the place we made for it, just as he took on, as one of his jobs, making dinner for the family. This division had been fine with us, or so I thought, until his comment made me weep—with gratitude for the kindness of it and hurt anger that not until he was on his way out the door had he acknowledged what I had contributed to our lives together.

So be it. But how strange it is what we withhold from one another. Is it that we take the making of a house for granted? Maybe. Until it is time to decide who gets the house, perhaps one of the most rancorous moments in most breakups these days.

I guess it used to be that the housewife kept the house to which she had been married, perhaps as much as to the husband, who was abandoning them both. He might have paid for it, but she breathed the day's life into it; and it was there that the children would continue to be raised. Thankfully we live in other times now; men are not cast out of their children's lives as frequently; women are not tied to their houses, either. It doesn't mean we have more clarity about how to proceed, though; there are no more rule books.

I ended up buying my husband's half of the house after a series of complicated psycho-emotional negotiations. I had found the house—or, more precisely, recognized its potential. I had fallen in love with it at first sight. I was taken with the forthright symmetry of its neo-colonial architecture: front door in the middle, windows, a whopping sixteen panes in each large frame, arranged on either side of the door, like a schoolchild's drawing of a house. Dark old wooden shingles, the bright contrast of the trim painted chalk white—outlining the shape of the house—black shutters, fat, simple columns, like old soda bottles, holding up balconies. Even a tiny sleeping porch clinging to the second story at the back. The house was nearly a hundred years old, and though it had been well loved by the previous owners, it had gone into a gentle decline that spoke of children having left home, money having gotten tighter, energy drawn down. The house had a fading elegance that drew me in immediately because I knew I could be of help. I knew exactly, instinctively, what needed to be done. I loved the feeling of the place: quiet, reserved, dignified in its poise. Nothing about it was showy, but it was beautifully built—hand-plastered walls, rare fruitwood floors—and its many qualities, though slow to reveal themselves, gave the house a strong presence. The gardens, too, looked promising, full of large old shrubs, towering trees, tangles of ivy—all well into old age and grown slightly out of control, a charming combination.

I had thrown myself into engineering the renovations

and the decoration with great enthusiasm. It often seems that one person shoulders the job of caring for a house, and takes on the endless tasks of furnishing, arranging, stocking up, and maintaining the luster of it all. I had been happy to be the one to do it. I had devoted hours to nursing camellias and azaleas and hydrangea and peonies and althea back to their bloom. And I had helped pay for it all, too. Of course, my husband had filled the house with the aroma of delicious food for friends and family; he had made his livelihood from the house, working from an office he had created in one of the bedrooms; he had indulged my wish to make it all as beautiful as possible, and he had helped pay for it, too.

Ultimately my success in contriving to stay planted in that house probably came down to the fact that I was completely incapable of even imagining moving to another house, let alone actually going out to look for one. I was paralyzed by the thought. I knew I would never find another house in that town that I could love as well.

After my husband moved out, I walked from one room to another, slowly, lingering in each doorway. That was where the painting of the ghostly man in the canoe had hung. That was where the armoire had stood, full of china for the next dinner party. Under that table had been a beautiful Persian rug. That was where I had once sat in a big, comfortable armchair and nursed my second son. Only the children's rooms had been left intact; the rest of the rooms were hollow, the walls ringing with memory. Each room bore the marks of hearts breaking—and our divorce had been an easy one, mutually agreed upon, finally, as the best solution to an

impossible sadness. But even if it was right, it was not pain-
less. I felt as if my heart were suspended over a vast emptiness.
And my house looked that way for a long time, too.

I went upstairs to the third-floor room that my husband
had used as his office. I had dragged a futon into it, intending
to sleep there because I couldn't imagine staying in the
master bedroom. I spent weeks, and then months, on that
futon, tossing and turning; it was worse during the nights
when the children stayed at his new house and I was alone,
and everything was too strangely quiet. I stayed there, on that
floor, in the spot where his desk had been, unable to move
back into what had been our room and was now to be my
room. I stayed for months, until I realized that I was behaving like an old dog whose master is long gone, and still she
sleeps by the fire next to the chair, waiting for a return, head
jerking up at every creaking floorboard.

I spent months simply looking at the shell of our marriage.
I felt alienated from the house; every room reminded me of
our lives there, and it seemed unfathomable, how to move on.
I felt as if I couldn't move at all; I felt listless, weary around
the house—everything seemed drab. I wondered about the
wisdom of staying there. It seemed impossible to move forward, to make the house just mine, just then; I couldn't see
how to rinse the tears from the air. Each room held an accusation of failure. There seemed very little to love about the
place, except for the pleasure the children took in returning
to their old rooms every week; that alone was fortifying. I
began to think about putting the house on the market and
forcing myself into a new setting.

It was during the time that I was too emotionally devastated to make a new home for myself—and for my children—that I began to think seriously about what it had meant to make a house, and a garden, at all. Houses and gardens express so much about ourselves, the state of our hearts, our lives. We all know that strange, uncomfortable feeling as we walk into a house in which something is wrong with the owners; we learn, over time, to read the cracks in the foundations by the way they zigzag up the walls. Ask the architects or decorators—anyone involved in the craft of building—and they'll tell you how easy it is to spot signs of structural and emotional collapse. If they're paying attention—and generally, they have to, for it falls to them to navigate, and then cover up, the shoals of the relationship—they can tell the state of a marriage by the interaction between their clients; sometimes they see the trouble before anyone else. Of course, it is always easier to spot someone else's fault lines.

But if our houses display the symptoms of our unease, they are also capable of showing us a way out of our troubles. Houses, if we take them seriously, and I do, are very demanding. You can leave them to disrepair only so long before the plaster starts raining down around your ears. And then you have to start paying attention.

Very late one early spring night, I sat in the only armchair left in the living room. Next to me was a candelabra, all four tapers burning to stubs. I had laid a fire and, in those small hours, the embers were glowing a smooth, silky orange. There was one other piece of furniture in the room, a table piled high with the books I was not interested in reading. I was listening to an opera, by Delibes, I think; I remember the music was grandiose and passionate and full of desperate, miserable longing. The French doors were open to the garden, it was cool outside, and unexpectedly, mingling with the music, came the sound of a fierce rainstorm. Gusts of damp air blew in the doors; the floors gleamed as lightning flashed. I could appreciate, all of a sudden, what was around me, in the wind, the hard rain, the thunder, and, too, in the crumbling plaster of the walls, the dark wood planks, the hot coals piled in the deep fireplace, the austere panes of glass in windows that glowed white with each crack of light. Beauty was all around. I was seeing it again for the first time since I had been on my own. I sat very still, taking in the spirit of the night, until I felt that I was in a place as holy as a church. And I was ready to be home.

BEDROOM Rx

I have always been sympathetic to the idea of taking to your bed when the going gets tough. It seemed like many of my friends were doing just that, sick of lovers, or husbands, or jobs, or just sick of everything. I felt homesick. I couldn't muster the energy to pull everything together again. I know plenty of people for whom a breakup is a battle cry for redecoration. For me, it brought on the existential crisis of decorating: what was the point?

What I really needed was to hibernate beneath the blankets, where most of us have spent a good amount of time. Bed is, paradoxically, where we might be surprised by our greatest happiness and haunted by our greatest despair. Some of us are confined to bed because of devastating illness—the cancers, brittle bones, strokes that hit with blunt and brutal energy and leave everyone in Job-like despair. Why him? Why her? Why me? Why? Dark thoughts. I was seeing too many loved ones suffer—or perhaps feeling their suffering more deeply, as mine was washing over me. So when I was finally ready to move off the futon on the floor in the old office, I went to my bedroom to heal.

The master bedroom. What an idea. I don't know how much incense I burned in an effort to appease the angry gods presiding over doomed love; they may have helped me, but the bedroom itself needed more than that. It was in pretty bad shape. For one thing, it was empty; I had gotten rid of all the furniture. For another, the walls had not been painted in years, and the plaster on the ceiling was badly cracked. Naturally the largest crack of all zippered right over the bed, and I had anxious fantasies of the ceiling collapsing on me while I slept. Major repairs were already underway in the living and dining rooms; I had hired painters to come in and fix walls and blanket everything in white, but I had intended to avoid the expense of having work done on the bedrooms; I guess I didn't believe in the master bedroom idea enough to commit money to it. So I decided to be a bit slapdash, much to the chagrin of the meticulous painter I had hired. Out of pity for my situation, I think—he used to cluck at me, every morning when he arrived, bringing in the paper, righting a trash can that had been knocked over during the night, how can a woman live without a husband?—the painter reluctantly agreed to skip the replastering and simply bandage the bedroom's wounded walls with a couple of coats of paint.

I had ripped a fashion ad out of a magazine that had been shot against striated walls of clay, in the open vein of a mine, perhaps. I paid no attention to the model or the dress; it was the background color that was extraordinary: dark, rich, comforting. A little somber, perhaps, but that seemed to match my mood. I was going to ground. I brought the ad to the paint store and asked for the closest thing to the color in the picture. Twelve quarts of botched attempts later—and a good deal more clucking about women alone—we got a match. My bedroom became a clay cave.

It may be that no man or woman is an island. Yes, we are all connected, sometimes in spite of our best efforts to shove off on our own. But what's wrong with islands? I would like to posit the homemaker's corollary to the dictum of the poet: All beds are islands—and pretty wonderful for refuge.

The old advice that you should spend time in your own guest room to see if it is properly outfitted is useful only if you know how to take care of yourself in the first place. Too many of us don't know how to treat ourselves well, almost as if we feel we don't deserve to, don't have time to, don't want to feel guilty about doing so. That's absurd; the bedroom should be utterly luxurious. If your marriage has gone bad, or your lover gone south, I say burn the sheets. And start over.

I added to a new mattress a featherbed I could sink into

deeply. I bought the best mattress I could find, figuring it cost less than a car and I was going to spend more time on it—even during my best days. I found the softest possible throw to drape around my shoulders or across my knees. No one is above having a security blanket on hand, at any age. The tiny hotel-fare side tables were gone. This time I moved in a big table and began to think of it as command central. (I had entered a battlefield, I knew, where my waking hours were those when the rest of the world was snugly asleep.) I made room for a dish as a resting place for a bottle of wine (or sparkling water or whiskey, or even hot milk), an old crystal goblet (why save the good stuff for dinner parties?), a sturdy lamp, a few rocks from my favorite beach, the silver candelabra that certainly wasn't being used in the dining room, an ancient, softly glazed porcelain cup and saucer, and the remote control for the music box. Whether it's Joni Mitchell or Gustav Mahler, you need all the music you can get, anywhere in the house that you are going to sit and listen. (I'm not big on so many speakers all over the house that you are in the world of surround sound—in other words, the world of malls, where music becomes background noise. Just put the music in the rooms in which you are going to pay attention.) In a gesture of real compassion, my baby brother surprised me with a visit from Los Angeles and undertook the wiring of my house for, as he said, *"son et lumière."* It was months after my new solitude and he understood how important music and movies would be to any recovery. He also knew that I would never have been able to shop for new equipment by myself, much less figure out how to plug it all in, so he did it for me. And so, too, he taught me my first big lesson in living alone: accept help. It was to be a long while before I learned the second lesson: ask for help.

I made sure there was at least one piece of art I loved, a painting of a rocky seashore, perched on the table so I could lay eyes on it when I woke up. And I picked several treasured books and piled them up on the table too, so that I would have the wisdom of the ancients on hand at any hour. Needless to say, all this activity took place in one of those air pockets in my depression, when I actually had the energy to do something. And afterward, I was exhausted from the hopefulness of the effort.

I'm told people don't like footboards anymore because they block the view of the TV. Move the television. It doesn't belong in the bedroom; you create your own drama there. I know, you can sit in bed and watch old movies. Like they do in new movies. The kind of movies that make you cry. Do you really need another source of tears in the bedroom? Footboards are good: the more the bed feels like a crib the more comforting it is. Sleigh beds, poster beds, *lits à la polonaises,* canopy beds, all create a world unto themselves. Even the modernist's version—the platform bed—keeps the demons at bay with its emphatic boundaries, like the edging in a garden. And those new beds with big, broad headboards that wrap all the way around the top and partway down the sides resemble nothing less than a good shoulder to cry on. (One hundred percent cotton on the sheets covering that shoulder would be nice, please. Egyptian, broadloom, polished, 350, whatever.)

Pain is inescapable. I knew there wasn't really a thing I could buy that would usher the pain out, much as I wished it. Even the best medicines don't work alone. The only way out of it is through it—with hope, perseverance, luck, wit, and a prayer. No matter how tiny (even the size of a pea) the pain may seem to others, our feelings about it are always large. We are sensitive to the lumps under our own mattresses. Sometimes there's no choice but to sleep it off. So you may as well sleep like a princess. And get better.

A LIFETIME OF CLOSETS

I have always been drawn to closets—my own hold as much fascination for me as do other people's (but I'm sorry to confess that I am an inveterate snoop). I seem to have invested a small fortune in large blue plastic stacking tubs and bubble wrap, and went through a few years during which I was constantly packing up the little knickknacks I had accumulated: rocks and sticks and birds' nests I could not stop bringing in from the countryside; bins of snapshots; small sculptures; teacups I was drawn to at every flea market

I visited. It was endless, the stuff I was squirreling away, and I wasn't buying any furniture to keep it in, much less display it on. I didn't want to look at my old possessions anymore. But even the new stuff I bought, for I never stopped haunting the shops, went straight into the closet. I began to realize that I simply liked closets; it comforted me to keep those small spaces neatly organized, clean, well stocked against future deprivation, and full of memories on which I could shut the door. It made me feel contained.

Rummaging around in my closets became a kind of therapy. I cannot remember a time when I wasn't fascinated by my mother's closets. I must have spent hours in them—and they were forbidden territory. Of particular interest to me were the piles of heavy old linen from France, thickly embroidered with mysterious initials, the kind no one used in the fifties because it was so inconvenient to launder; old silver—knife rests, salt cellars, oyster forks, napkin rings, unidentifiable utensils—the kind no one used because it was so inconvenient to polish; family photographs, some, strangely, with the faces cut out, in old leather albums, the kind no one used anymore because of the inconvenience of pasting in all those corners; serious suits from the forties with big silky labels from boutiques in Paris and Casablanca, flirtatious beyond my imagining (my mother?) in their décolletage, of a size no longer worn after the inconvenience of having borne four babies. . . . What was I looking for? Nothing in particular. Just everything. Who was she? Where did she come from? Who was I? Where did I come from? My mother was filled with secrets, and I looked in her closets to unravel her mystery.

Many women are drawn to their mother's closets (and why do a family's closets always seem to belong to the mother?). I stumbled on this secret time after time; how often has a friend confessed that her husband simply cannot understand why she has to come back from every visit to her parents' house with shopping bags full of stuff. Not even stuff she needs, just stuff she had to have. The things I wanted most of all from my mother's closets were the bed linens and a tall, elegant silver vase I had unearthed in there. I begged and was denied for decades. I understand now that my mother could not part easily with the only reminders of her life in another world. But by the time she relented, the silver vase had a nasty dent in its side, having fallen against a sharp edge and been left crammed for too long in that uncomfortable position; the linens were yellowed, decaying from disuse. Even things need a life.

What is everyone looking for when we rummage in attics, flea markets, consignment stores, thrift shops, estate sales, antiques galleries? Antiques are marvelous time capsules; their line and ornamentation reflect an era's sensibility about wealth and beauty, whether Rococo or Regency. We respond to particular things because we feel a kinship with the time from which they sprang. And we can measure how our tastes change, develop, by the periods of antiques through which we move. A piece of furniture can be its own storehouse of secrets—or revelations. But captured, as well, in the material of the thing is the craft of the artisan, the touch of a human hand. I will never forget a ninety-year-old dealer in New Orleans who showed me how to read for age in an antique. He pressed my hand over the flawless plane of a table and dragged my fingers across unseen ripples of cherry, finding in the undulations the Braille left behind by moisture, heat, bugs, time.

When I had my babies, I read their heads with my hands, feeling my way across bumps and dents, swelling bruises, hot foreheads, and cool cheeks. I studied the hue of pupil and the fuzz of hair and I found in them the eyes of a beloved grandmother or the rich mane of a wild cousin. We watch, as our babies age, the way they walk, or sit, or put their hands on their hips, or shrug a shoulder, and we see an animated imprint of a grandfather or an aunt. One day, while packing boxes of photo albums, I came upon a photo of my oldest son at the age of seven leaping off a cliff into the ocean. His posture of joy, in midair, hands thrown up, fingers spread, was identical to that of his father, caught in a photograph at the same age, leaping in glee down a sand dune. Living with the past. It is impossible to avoid.

I told a friend about this bit of accidental tourism into my past, and he counseled me to stop looking back. But it isn't that I wanted to live in the past; that seems a dry and dusty path to wander. I don't believe in the past perfect, and don't yearn to return to any particular moment. One of the benefits of growing older, it seems, is a greater comfort with the simple present. It is from that vantage point that we find beauty in the accumulation of details. "Live in the layers, / Not on the litter" writes the poet Stanley Kunitz. His desk overlooks a compost heap in his garden. The layering takes a long time; just as true of people as of things. For the past is what we have made of our lives, and to have a past—and to learn from it, honor it, and celebrate it—is a great luxury.

BUBBLE CATHEDRALS

You know how you're never, ever supposed to use bubble bath in a whirlpool tub with the jets on? Well, I've done it, and the effect is irresistible. The jets whip the soap up to such heights that you can simply disappear under glittering piles of bubbles.

There must be some genetic coding for bubble play. All bathing children I have ever observed mold bubbles onto their bodies to see what they would look like with beards, bosoms, long hair, and funny hats. My play is architectural—

the fun of the great bubble cliffs is pushing and shaping them into pillars and archways, and carving rooms out of their airy depths. Because the bubbles are so high, you feel like you are inside a crystal building. Bubble cathedrals. Bubbles are like the glitter in the sidewalk, or ice crystals shimmering on the window, caught in a shaft of weak winter sunlight: they're magic.

We all find magic in different parts of our homes. The bathroom, for a few years, was easily one of my favorite rooms. I had spent a great deal of time, during the renovation of the house, thinking about what was important in the design of the fixtures for the bathrooms. I'm a tub person, an oddity in a nation of shower people. Taking a hot bath is one of the most relaxing and gentle ways to begin and end a day. I think a tub should be roomy, but it is not a pool, and you are not a mermaid in a fountain. You want to be in the water, not floating across it.

I had had a window put in at the foot of the tub, and quite by chance it perfectly framed the gnarled limb of an old oak tree growing at the end of the garden. I watched, from my hot bath, that branch turn vermillion in the fall, chartreuse in the spring; I traced its crooked line across the white winter skies. Every once in a while (and if I were of a more scientific bent I could have predicted when, but then I would have lost the surprise) I could take a bath late at night by the light of a full moon hanging fatly in the window. I never sprang for a hot tub outside, but I love the idea of it. So I fill my bath with very hot water and throw open the window and watch the steam rise. This is especially pleasing on cold winter evenings. (One of my best housekeeping tips: when you are done with your bath, keep the tub full, all day or all night, of that fragrant water you have just poured. It humidifies the bedroom, and the scent suffuses the air and lingers throughout the house. There's nothing like waking in the middle of the night in a glade of lavender, or coming home to a field of verbena.)

I filled my bathroom with all the things that make other rooms inviting: a comfortable armchair; a soft rug; a table to hold special things; a large vase sitting on the floor, full of fragrant flowers; candles burning; a pile of books and magazines. The best thing I did was to start ripping pages from magazines and pinning to the walls poems and paragraphs and pictures that moved me, made me think, caught my breath. Having something to read by the mirror over the sink makes me slow down. Had it been possible, I would have put a fireplace in that bathroom.

I do not have jets in my tub at home—I don't like bathing in turbulent waters, as a rule, and I don't like bumps against my back. (I guess I didn't mind violating the hotel's rules and playing in the bubble cathedrals.) I like my own tub to be quiet, with a thin film of foam across the top of the water and time for a long soak. The tub is a great place for tears when you're grown up and living alone; when you're a teenager (or you aren't alone but need to be), the shower drowns out your sobs and drums out eavesdropping ears.

My bathroom became so inviting that my sons decided they wanted to use it, too. Bucking the trend for his and her versions of everything, we began a life of ours. It was comforting to huddle together in the bathroom. I sat in the arm-chair and read to my youngest son while he lounged under oil slicks thick as Alaskan spills; he liked to mix his own lavish formulas from my stockpile of bath stuff. Theo was not yet modest about his bathing, and the warm water seemed to relax him into conversation as well. We talked about every-thing, in those days, especially his favorite questions: Why are we here? What is the point of life? My older son, Alex, liked me to set everything up and leave him alone: candles lit; warmed towels piled on the chair; music playing softly; tub steaming; door firmly shut; privacy, please. I loved this ritual, being able to arrange it for him and seeing that it gave him solace, especially in the first year after the divorce, when he became quiet and introspective and careful about every move he made.

It was in the bathroom that I quickly became aware of what I was up against, raising two boys by myself half the week. Not to imply their father wasn't involved—he was. But each of us was on our own, under separate roofs, and that was perhaps the strangest and most upsetting thing about the divorce. No way to compare notes in a hurry, no way to correct course quickly because someone notices some-thing when the other one isn't paying attention. And who sees everything? We had given up the chance for reprieve, for those small moments of respite from daily child duties—traded for half a week of total deprivation of child care—and we had given up the chance for complicity. The bathroom was obviously a place where boundaries about bodies and privacy got negotiated, and then renegotiated, pretty quickly. I would have liked advice, another opinion, about how boys grow up. At the same time, it seemed important to me to try to raise boys who had some appreciation of life's sensual pleasures, as well as some knowledge about how to relax, unwind from the day. I encouraged bathroom time.

We respected each other's privacy always, without locks or doors banging. There was a tacit understanding that if we were going to share such close quarters, we had better be gentle about crossing paths. Each one of us cherished the privacy and peace of the bathroom. Indeed, it seems to have become a favorite retreat because it is a room that can be many things to many people. I got a phone call late one night from a friend in Boston. She really wanted a high-security heart-to-heart, and her children really wanted just one more glass of water, one more tuck of the blankets, one more reassurance, before sleep. Harried, she took her portable phone from one room to another—kitchen to library to hallway to bedroom. Interruption upon interruption, and she was frantic. Then things got quiet, and she was able to talk and I to listen quietly. At the end of the conversation I asked her where she had finally settled down. "You'll never guess where I found a private place," she said. "In the bathroom." She was sitting in the tub—no water—with the glass doors pulled shut. Bathroom as phone booth.

GARDEN PATHS

D o all gardeners have a first garden, a garden that turned them into gardeners? I don't mean a primal patch of land, but the experience of tending a plant or shaping a flower bed or dividing a root that suffuses you with a "this is what it's all about" feeling of pleasure, peace, or bone-tiredness. What really gets us started down the gardening path? For me, the experience occurred when I was very young and it colored my expectation of what it means to make a garden.

I am the child of a country boy from Kentucky and a city lady from Casablanca. My father, being an outdoor type, was (and is) in a constant state of agitation about something that needs tending, mending, patching, or pruning. My mother was (and is) a decidedly indoor person. She finds it almost unnatural to commune with nature, something best done poolside. I was so impressed with her model of what a lady did and did not do that I remember to this day the shock of coming upon a girlfriend's mother—a grown-up woman probably as old as I am now—on her hands and knees in the dirt, weeding. I had never seen a woman in that position before, although I was at least ten or twelve years old at the time. I immediately loved what it meant to garden: the first time I could legitimately get my hands dirty.

When I was four years old, my father launched what was to become a five-year project: the cutting and clearing of paths through the woods to the stream that ran along the backyards in our suburban development. This seemed a very grand project to me, for the woods looked impenetrable and the distance to the water vast. But, determined to be at my father's side despite any obstacle, I took up my tiny rake and shovel.

The idea was to create several kinds of trips to the river— the straight path, the fat path, the very skinny path, the crooked path, and a few others. In such a limited space, these paths had to overlap, and the trick was to be clever about how and when they crisscrossed and what might happen if you started down the straight path, say, and then turned onto the crooked one. Once the route was traced and shaped and cut and cleared, we began the business of placing stone markers and creating rails out of split branches found on the ground and laying logs down to make stairs and then sandwiching plants into all the spaces between the paths. We put pansies in sunny clearings; I remember vividly my mother explaining that they were her favorite flowers because they had a good attitude: they always turned their faces to brightness. She told me also that in Morocco, geraniums were the flowers of silliness, and it was high-spirited to have lots of them around the house.

My father was drawing a garden up out of the backyard, though I didn't have a clue to that at the time. He is a surgeon. His has been a busy life. But I don't remember ever resenting the time he wasn't home, because when he was with us he was present, delightedly engaged. When we were digging out those paths, we were so close, so connected in the work we had undertaken together, so serious in our play that I was nurtured for a long time by the reverberations of that activity. Those paths took me somewhere far beyond that river.

A few years ago, I went to visit my father as he recuperated from open-heart surgery. Paths of surgical staples crisscrossed his body, traveling up his leg, across his belly and chest, down his arm. It is a surgeon's job to cut through a body. I have often wondered at the sheer nerve it takes to slice into human flesh with a scalpel, to trace a precise and irreversible course through skin and muscle. It takes some presumption, too, to cut into the earth and to reshape and redefine—to alter the natural course of things, to commit to having planted a seed, to start a path with no idea, really, where it will lead.

The gardening I began to do as an adult became one of those solitary pleasures. The more time I spent alone out there, the more alone I became. I was finally gardening to be alone, and yet I knew it wasn't the only way to garden. I am convinced that some of gardening's magic happens in the collaboration, in the "not you, not me, but us" scheme of life. Sometimes gardens give you a measure of your desire (or capacity) for company, sometimes they clue you in to your need for time alone. And gardens are as much about the work that goes into them as they are about the results; I'm disdainful of the mega-rich program of transplanting ancient trees and mature privet and getting instant drama. It seems a shallow, showy version of gardening; it misses the point.

I don't remember much about what my childhood backyard ended up looking like; I am not sure I ever saw it, exactly, as a whole. My focus was on the experience of making that garden, and it was in that way very particular, very small in its view. The fascinating thing about gardening is that it is an activity that is at once companionable and solitary, deeply solitary. There is something about the concentration it requires that shuts out the world, or distills it into the small things at hand. You may as well be trying to empty the ocean with a teaspoon, for all the permanence your hard work will have. Still it compels. Just as I carry forever a memory of digging side by side with my father, so, too, I garden rapt in my dreams, wandering in my thoughts along some path to which I have not found an end.

OLD GARDEN

Moving back to New York from Texas, a married woman, and a new mother, I had some difficulty accepting the idea that it was time to buy a house on the outskirts of the city, in Westchester, and ride a train to work every day in another town that was not where my babies napped. Some nights I would get home and stand, in the fading light, at the bottom of the driveway, looking up at the house in disbelief, tears running down my face. What had I done with my life? I had given up on the vibrant disorder of city life, and taken on the dull trappings of suburban life. Worse. I had become the kind of working woman who needed to wear sneakers with her suit just to be able to walk to the train station. I had become the Woman in the Gray-Flannel Suit. A commuter. A cliché.

Gardening became my way of growing into the new life—digging in for the long haul, connecting, committing to a patch of soil, rooting in and under and around and through it all. I began to spend countless hours with my hands in the earth. It was not unusual for me to head into twilight with my garden chores on a Saturday or Sunday—or both. There was simply so much to do. A tangled but fascinating wood-land garden in front of the house needed rescuing; it had been put in generations earlier, judging by azaleas towering eight feet over me, grown leggy and clogged with ivy and creeper. Towering over that garden was a stand of sassafras trees, the most awkward-looking trees I had ever seen. There must be thirty or forty of them; strange, but I have never counted. They are gangly; no limbs branch out from the trunks until they are at least two stories high, and then there are very few branches. But the bark is deeply etched and patterned, and the rows of trunks are pleasing to look at from the living room window. The trees make a protective canopy over the azaleas, which bloom with a pure whiteness every spring, right around Mother's Day. When I look down from my bedroom window, the garden seems to be filled with drifts of snow mounding and undulating gracefully through the front yard. In the autumn, the sassafras leaves fall and begin to rot, and the house is swathed in the scent of an exotic, long-forgotten tea. This balm works miracles on the azaleas.

I was told by a Realtor that one of the reasons the house had been on the market for so long was that it had no "curb appeal." Surely if I bought it I would cut down many of the trees, open it up, let in light, have a lawn. As far as I was concerned, the less curb appeal the better. The sassafras hid the house from view; they were so effective a screen that I never needed to hang curtains. Naturally, the first thing I did after we moved in was to prune and fertilize the trees, and begin selectively nursing the new shoots that were coming up so that they would rise up in good health as the next generation of the garden.

Much of the backyard was overrun, too, with bitter, honeysuckle, grapevine, and my favorite pest, pokeweed. There are great rewards in mucking about with old gardens—the discovery of mature but long-forgotten plants, for one. I took a pirate's pleasure in untangling from a hillock of chokeberry what turned out to be a ten-foot-tall *Camellia japonica*—a glossy-leaved treasure I recognized from visits to New Orleans. Startling, as camellias aren't supposed to live in my wintry zone. Camellias were a plant very much admired by my in-laws. So I felt my garden was making a karmic connection to the family I had joined in marriage. I took my cues about the character of what would become the new garden from what I unearthed of the old one.

And, of course, there had to be new gardens. Gardeners have an insatiable desire for new beds; things always look like they could use a few more plants, a few more feet. I carved more and more out of the lawn. Whatever I was doing out there, though, I was always at peace.

And then it was time to dismantle the household. I stayed planted. It was winter. The days were short, and I came home in the dark. When spring came, slowly that year, I did not head out into the garden to chop apart the hardened mulch, open the beds, and inspect for those tender green shoots as I had every year before. Spring became summer, and still I stayed put. I simply could not take care of the garden any longer. It held no magic, promised no peace. It had been for us; we were no longer, so what was the use? I let it go. It flourished without me. It even seemed to take care of its own weeds, burying them under luscious new growth. Fall came, the sedum flushed, the hydrangea dried in gigantic bronze bouquets. The garden put itself down for the winter, and all I did was watch. Too sad and too busy and too confused to do a thing.

But the garden went on. A few more springs passed in the same sorry state, and then one day I noticed a profusion of weeds and decided to do something about them. Weed. I noticed dead branches, and decided to do something about that. Prune. I noticed gaps, and went to fill them. Plant. I noticed languor, and thought I'd relocate some things to sunnier climes. Transplant . . . Divide. Fertilize. Water. I didn't have the heart to do much, but I did some. Enough. Enough to get by, enough to get going again. As I worked, I thought how I would never (why do I still say never?) be able to pour heart and soul into that garden again, but that it would be a lovely thing to maintain it, just until the next gardener moved in to renew it.

How striking it is to be able to measure a passage of time in increments of weeding and pruning and planting. It dawned on me: I had tended that garden in great, lavish, loving strokes. It had given me quiet, steady, demanding, and undemanding seasons of pleasure. I took care of the garden, then the garden took care of me.

THE CHOSEN FAMILY

It was my mother-in-law who taught me that it was fine to love your house. My own mother could not have been more distant from the whole subject of decorating; my parents bought their house, along with all the furnishings, from a man who was obsessed with the color green, and green everything stayed nearly the entire time I was growing up. Why would anyone spend money to change perfectly decent furniture? My mother cared about music, and pianos, and good table manners, and proper behavior. I loved books;

she was constantly knocking them from my hands, with the warning that I would ruin my eyes. Maybe she was right. But her resentment of anything that took me away from the keyboard was fierce. She eventually, reluctantly, succumbed to the primacy of homework, only because good grades might help me with an application to a good conservatory. My mother's single-minded and passionate devotion to the practice of the piano troubled me enormously as a child; her expressiveness was hard for someone of my quieter temperament to take, and eventually I wanted nothing but to find peace.

The first time I saw my future in-laws' house in New Orleans, I felt I had walked into a house I was meant to love. The house was entirely made of brick and huge planes of glass. It was a perfect box, entrance door in the middle of a brick wall, a colonnade of arches across the front porch. (There was the symmetry that I would years later respond to in my own house.) Where the front wall of the house was solid, the back wall was glass, sheltered by another colonnade of brick arches. The sensation of moving quickly from mystery to transparency was thrilling. Uplifting. How could there be anything but clarity in such a place?

The center of the box was cut out to create an atrium, so that as soon as you opened the front door to go inside you once again had the outdoors in view. In the atrium a fountain bubbled and splashed over a grid laid out in cobblestone. The front and the back of the house were embraced by the gigantic limbs of live oak trees, limbs that seemed to defy gravity and hang for many meters parallel to the ground. The house was filled with light, the walls were covered with art, and at least three rooms were lined with books. It was hushed; how could anyone raise their voices in such a place—the walls themselves would have shattered. To my naïve eyes, strife in that house was unthinkable. This was an architecture that must determine civil living, and it was where I wanted to be. I felt I had found the home in which I was meant to live.

We all have the family into which we are born. And then we have the families we choose, or who choose us. My husband's family was most definitely a family to which I felt I belonged. There were, indeed, times I thought I fell in love with all of them when I fell in love with him. His sister was a close friend, his father was a charming, eccentric, mysterious fellow. But it was his mother who held the most appeal for me.

Barbara was a devoted and energetic psychiatric social worker. She was also a great patron of the contemporary arts scene in New Orleans and she was a popular person who cultivated strong and enduring friendships. She was politically engaged, and in the midst of a Republican enclave she held fast to her Democratic ideals, a Jew who mingled freely with the Catholic community.

This woman who was so smart, and so involved in her community—really, as feminist a role model as you could find in her generation—used to say to me, "You know, I'm really just a hausfrau. I love nothing better than to take care of my house, to furnish it, to shop for it, to set a beautiful table, to know that everything is in its place." She had come from a simple, middle-class family, the daughter of a small-town doctor in New Jersey, and married into great wealth; when she arrived in New Orleans she was overwhelmed at the challenge of running a household with servants, and with an expectation that things be maintained at a sophisticated level. She adapted well. She would often describe her first meetings with an interior decorator, a man flown in from New York to "do" the house she and her husband had built. They were modernists in a city that found such design horrifying; their house was considered scandalous. To this day, and by now I have looked at many houses, theirs is one of the most beautiful works of architecture I have seen.

When her son and I set up our first house in Texas, Barbara was the one who helped me shop for upholstered furniture, antiques, art, plates, and glasses, all manner of things. She was indefatigable in the hunting and gathering, and her enthusiasm was contagious. She had me hooked. What's more, our errands would be laced with conversation about the political news of the day, about psychological theories concerning my children's development, about what was happening on the public art front. So I learned that you didn't have to be a dope to be a hausfrau, and that, for as strident a feminist as I was in those days, was an important thing to learn. Barbara was my closest friend at a critical time in my life. When my oldest son was born, he fell in love with Barbara the first time she held him in her arms, sitting on a sofa she had helped me choose, against pillows she had sent because she loved their vibrant colors. She looked vibrant, with her first grandchild in her lap. She and Alex had a profound and instantaneous bond; it seemed almost chemical. (Later, my younger son was to have the same immediate connection with my mother. I remember the same deep kinship with my father's mother. Sometimes the bonds we create hardly seem a matter of choice.)

Barbara and I talked about everything and everyone. How could I not have understood what it meant, that the only thing I couldn't talk to her about was our unhappiness in our marriage? But I talked to no one.

And how did I not notice, for many years, that her house was too quiet, that conversation among family members was cordoned off from certain kinds of subjects? How did I not notice that there was never music in the air, that a burden of judgment about everything and everybody hung over our heads, that there was no room for spontaneous activity in that ordered household? An architecture that had measured civility now seemed to have confined emotion. I didn't want to see anything except perfection; any shortcoming was mine. The fact is, I still feel this way. My mother-in-law had constructed for herself and her family a life of high standards. My mistake—the same as hers—was to expect perfection.

When my husband and I broke up, he flew to New Orleans to tell his parents, and I drove to Connecticut to tell mine. My mother-in-law told me, over the phone, that she was furious and disappointed. With ruthless judgment, she had decided that the failure of the marriage was mine, and because of it she would never be able to love me again. I was devastated, and the loss of her friendship became a large part of the wound of the divorce. I lost two families when our marriage split apart. But I never lost the passion she kindled in me for homemaking, and in a way—though I wouldn't understand it for many years—she gave me the tools of the hausfrau that would help me forge my way out of my grief.

Barbara and I did not speak for years. I saw her again when she and her husband flew to New York for our son's bar mitzvah. By then my ex-husband was with the woman he would soon marry. The instant Barbara and I laid eyes on each other we burst into tears. She was in a wheelchair. I bent to put my arms around her frail body—how much she had aged—and we held each other for a few moments. I somehow knew that I would never see her again after that. But I was sure that she still loved me, as I loved her, always.

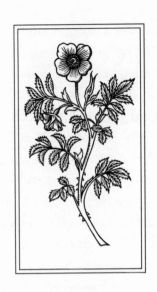

TAKE A SEAT

There are certain pieces of furniture I had insisted on keeping during the negotiations over household division. One of them is an old garden bench we had moved with us to New York from Texas. I could never part with it, and it was as difficult and wonderful to have in my life as my upright piano, for like the piano, I had to haul that bench from house to house, garden to garden, and always find a place for it, because it could never be replaced. That bench meant a great deal to me, but I had forgotten exactly why until, one unusually warm spring day, I had stayed home from work, alone with a child who felt too sick to go to school. I was glad for the break. We rested outside, and suddenly, as I was gazing at the bench, it came back to me, a memory from ten years earlier.

It had happened in the garden.

Texas. I was home from work too early: this time I was the one sick with flu. It was a fine winter day, as I recall, the kind you get in Austin. Balmy. As soon as the sitter saw me, she went home; she, too, was sick. So I was alone with the baby. My fifteen-month-old, firstborn son. Still in office mode, busy, bossy, restless, I herded him and eighty toys into the backyard, thinking the sunshine would do us good. Alex was always cheerfully tolerant of my suggestions of Things to Do, but he usually ignored me and went his own way. That afternoon was no exception. As he firmly toddled off to poke with a stick at a clump of grass, I felt my temperature rise and then thought, Relax. Take a seat.

The seat was the long, heavy wooden bench—the classic English sort to which I always brought lots of cushions. The teak was silvered with age, green in spots with lichen, rubbed by bodies, bleached by rain, snow, sun, stained with wine and finger paints, nicked and bruised by errant wagons, lawn mowers, tree limbs . . . its patina our history.

In Austin, the bench sat under a large wooden pergola, which was supported by six massive, round, stuccoed columns resting on a slabby floor of yellow limestone. At the foot of each column I had planted clematis and trumpet vine, "Mme. Galen"; the young sprouts were making their speedy way up. I lay down on the bench and watched my son, busy and quietly absorbed. He wandered nearer, and I began again, reflexively, nervously, uselessly, with the insecurity of a new mother, to wonder how I would keep him entertained in my weakened state. But something caught his eye as he approached, so he, too, took a seat, squatting, with his little back against a sturdy bench leg.

I saw that he had spotted a lizard, a tiny thing, vivid green, ruby-throated, its long, thin, padded toes gripping the column, its body absorbing the heat of sun on stucco. "Lizard," I said helpfully, always looking to make a point. Alex ignored me. He wasn't much of a conversationalist. To be honest, he had hardly started talking at all. That was something else for me to fret about. "Bench," I went on, determined. Still working it. "Plant. Dirt. Lizard. Boy." (This last an excuse for a little nudge into the boy's irresistibly chubby paunch.) He did not take his eyes off the lizard. I finally realized he was spellbound, and I shut up. The lizard's sides pulsated with life, in and out. My child breathed in and out. I breathed in and out, raspily. No one moved. Time passed us by. I felt the last of the day's tension ease out of my body.

Years later, now caring for the ten-year-old boy, those moments on the garden bench came back to me, and I realized that gardening has to be as much about contemplation as it is about tilling and toiling. Mental tilling, perhaps. A way to slow down time, for yourself, or for you and someone else, so that you can reconnect with something deeper, something that lies under and around the day-to-day— something, perhaps, in one another. Turning things over, quietly thinking, in a place that gives you a peaceful corner for just a moment or two. A place, a seat in a place, in which you are comfortable and free enough to simply let go.

My own reverie that Texas afternoon was shattered by a wild shriek from my son, who rocketed up and threw his arms skyward. I was certain he had been stung by a bee, but his cries were joyful. As I swept him into my arms, he pointed at the lizard skittering up the column, and the words came tumbling out. "Bye-bye, lizard! Bye-bye!" His first sentence.

What a triumph. How could I ever give that bench away? I would carry it to the ends of the earth. It isn't just a piece of furniture. It helped me stop time. How grateful I am. I caught a first bloom from my late bloomer in that garden. I paused, in the embrace of that bench, enough to take in the moment, and it will be mine forever.

LOST AND FOUND

One of the results of joint custody—which could be renamed disjointed custody—is that you split up vacation time. The first summer we were apart, the children headed off to their father's new house in the mountains and I was left alone in a little house by the sea in Rhode Island that we had rented for half a dozen years as a family. I felt abandoned.

Being at the house plunged me into a torpor of memories. I could not stop thinking about everything that had happened in its rooms, in the garden where babies learned to walk, or run, or play hide-and-seek—my youngest son had come to this house for the first time when he was six months old—at the harbor where my husband would greet the fishing boats early in the morning, and bring home that night's dinner. When I was in the ill-fated marriage I craved the relief of ending the struggle to make things right. That came, sweetly at first, and then all I wanted was to retrieve the things that had been right all along—the things that ultimately hadn't been strong enough ballast to keep us steady, but that I had cherished nonetheless. The beach house had been a place where the peaceful domestic rituals had reigned—hanging wet bathing suits on the old clotheslines, grilling in the back-yard, sleeping under heavy quilts that kept out the chilly night air. It marked one of the seasons of our lives together, and that rhythm had been disrupted. Now the place that had given me such happiness was threatening to swamp me in despair. I couldn't imagine leaving the community, not hav-ing it in my life, for its incomparable beauty still moved me. But I felt immune to any respite the house itself offered. Somehow it stirred up in me all the longing I could ever feel for the lost life. All I wanted was to forget.

Late every afternoon I walked the mile down the road to the beach club. At the end of the day the lifeguards would have retired to their rooms, the sun would be slanting across the water, and I would be free to take a long, forbidden swim out around the pink granite cliffs that bordered the cove. I am a creature of habit, and in times of trouble I cling especially close to routines; they give a comforting structure to days that threaten to cave in. People's habits overlap, and I had come to recognize neighbors who daily took the same walk at the same time. One was an older woman who for years had nodded a friendly hello as I passed her on the road.

I saw her again one afternoon as I set off for my swim. She was heading away from the beach, but she didn't respond to my greeting. I figured she was distracted, and I was, too. Halfway to the beach, I realized I had forgotten my cap and goggles. I turned around to retrieve them. I passed the woman again; she, too, had turned around to go the other way. I nodded hello and her gaze still seemed abstracted. I passed her on my way back out to the beach a second time; she had changed direction yet again. This time she smiled and looked at me quizzically, so I held up my goggles and called out an explanation for my hasty return trip and then added, kiddingly, "Did you forget something, too?" An odd look flashed across her face, a shadow of fear, and she replied simply, "I forget where I live. I am lost."

In spite of all the years I had passed her on the street, I had no idea who this person was. That's the way this community operates; it is considered polite to respect one another's privacy and you simply expect that, eventually, someone will make an introduction; otherwise it is unnecessary. The custom has never seemed unfriendly to me, quite the opposite. But now I was at a loss as to what to do, for the woman standing in front of me, though not at all a stranger, had no idea who she was. Neither did I.

She had been wandering back and forth on the road for a

couple of hours, she told me. "I've taken this walk so many times. Everything looks familiar, and then that melts. I can't remember anything. I don't know where I am. I cannot find my way home."

Assuming she couldn't have walked very far, and remembering that I'd always seen her on a particular stretch of the road, I offered to walk with her and start knocking on doors. She came along with me and stood off to the side, docile, quiet, registering not so much as a trace of recognition as I stepped up to each door. Of course most people weren't home—those who were shook their heads gently and said no, she didn't belong to them, theirs was not her house. No one recognized her, either, but July was the month for summer rentals and we were all vaguely familiar strangers.

The woman seemed to be growing very sad, and she began to tell me about taking her walk, how she had done it for years and years, how things had changed along the way, trees blown away by winds, gardens washed out by floods, houses damaged by storms, children knocked off the road by so many fast cars, everything grown busier and more terrible. She was wandering in a world of haphazard violence, but she insisted she had never felt afraid during her walk. She seemed only bemused now at finding herself so lost. We tried a few more doors with no luck. I was beginning to wonder what I was going to do when we ran out of houses; nothing sparked the slightest flicker of response in her eyes, not a driveway, a hedge, a bed of flowers, the color of the trim or the shutters on the windows. I knocked at every door on the street anyway, and finally a woman opened one and said, flatly, "Oh, there she is; we were wondering when she would come home. . . ." I explained that she had been walking up and down a good while, hours, quite lost, and the woman sighed, defeated, and said, "Alzheimer's. It seems to come and go. She needs to walk. She needs the exercise. She loves the water, but we can't let her swim anymore. She just goes to the beach, gets in, and starts swimming for the horizon. She is so stubborn and so strong it has become almost impossible to stop her."

I was left to ponder this drama as I made my way once again to the beach. I was shocked, first, by the dulled response to the woman's arrival home; I would have been in a panic of loss had someone I loved vanished on a walk. Then again, I hadn't been living with anyone's pattern of disappearances, though it was dawning on me that disappearing was exactly what I had been yearning to do. I could not grasp the full weight of what I had just heard from the old woman, how horrible it was to be so lost that you could not even recognize where you lived. Your home. I remembered getting lost as a young child, several times, being separated from my parents in a large, frenetic crowd. I was stricken with the terror of finding myself so hopelessly alone in the world. But that was not the same as standing at your own front door without a clue as to where you were.

The beach was empty when I got there. I looked out over the sea and toyed with the idea of heading for the horizon and not turning back. What would that be like? I turned my gaze back to the shore and one of the wooden backboards, propped up in the sand for people to lean against as they read or dozed, caught my eye. The evening light had revealed a greasy, faint, but perfectly intact stain left on the board by someone's sun-lotioned back; I looked closer and saw a family of backs. There were the man's thicker, heavier muscles, neatly, precisely outlined, and there were a couple of smaller patches next to him. It was eerie, unnerving. I felt as if I had found the kind of tracing people see on cave walls, or screen doors, apparitions of Jesus, of Mary, the sort of shadowy thing that, if you squint the right way, might give you an intimation of immortality. But this shadowy presence was weirdly fleshy, and it was calling me in an earthly direction. You cannot forget, it seemed to say. You do not want to forget. That would be truly terrible. Find your way home.

I got in the water and swam for the horizon, strong strokes pulling me out quickly, and just for a moment I liked the feeling of heading straight out. Just for a moment. Then I turned for a long, long swim, and I kept the shore in sight with every breath.

HOME ALONE

What she wanted—what she had planned on—was to fall in love, get married, and make a home with someone. It wasn't happening, though. (Maybe she didn't really want it to; certainly it could have, there had been possibilities, but they were never quite right.) She was a person of accomplishment, fortitude, and sophistication. As she muscled her way into her forties, she began to feel hanging in the air the distinct staleness that comes with living too long like a college student: street-find furniture, plank-and-block bookcases.

But my friend was having a tough time giving herself permission to go ahead, buy a place, decorate, live well. She who never took no for an answer at work seemed paralyzed when it came to telling herself yes. As if going ahead on her own meant shutting the door on the hope of finding true love. But the day finally came to close on her first home, a home she was prodded into buying by an accountant who firmly showed her how much money she was wasting in rent, perhaps the only argument not lost on her. I was ready to uncork a bottle of champagne; my friend burst into tears.

"I never thought I would be doing this alone."

Well, most of us didn't. At best we are of two minds about being alone. We're from a generation, feminist and post, that grew up saying we needed men like fish needed bicycles (a phrase that seems so quaint now, and naïve, but charming in its zany defiance). I for one was such an ardent feminist through my high school years that in (an admittedly subtle) rebellion, I decided I would be damned if I would wait to be a bride to choose my china pattern and so bought my first porcelain teacups (Royal Worcester) to take with me to college. (God forbid that I should forgo china simply because I was living in a dormitory.) While I was at it, I started a pattern for my best friend. (Twenty-odd years later, we are both still adding to those patterns; for someone who does a lot of cooking for one, I have enough china to serve platoons of dinner guests.) Now we are a generation that has watched abandonment tear a jagged edge through our lives—whether through death, divorce, or utter confusion about all our choices. What we assemble, however painstakingly, we also disassemble. However devastatingly.

It is hard for many to go it alone—and of course this is just as true for men as it is for women. Forget all the spiritual crises; let's just focus on the little picture. Fussing around with fabrics, alone. Picking the paint color, alone. Rearranging the furniture, alone. It's like doing therapy, alone: there is no one to say, "You're talking a lot about blue, but you seem more excited when you get to green; are you sure you're not avoiding ... ?" No one to suffer with over the reality checks—you know, the ones that you write to pay for the Oushak and the Directoire chair. And the mortgage. No one to applaud and appreciate the daily effort.

Of course, you can find yourself doing all these things alone even when you are not alone, which is even worse.

My tearful friend finally gave herself permission to live in a style to which she immediately became accustomed. She hired a talented decorator; with true executive aplomb, she speedily groomed her first home. I have been watching another friend take an entirely different tack; she has been settling into her house for the last decade, carefully, methodically reupholstering, rearranging, repainting. She could easily afford to hire someone to help, but has chosen instead to strip and sand years of old paint from handsome wooden doors by herself. Her work is deliberate, conscientious. I think of her as fitting into her place the way water slowly carves and smoothes its way into stone.

And me? There I was, home alone, too. Coming at it from the other direction. Years into my divorce, I had let my house go; I had turned my back on its needs and it seemed to be waiting quietly to talk again. Houses are patient with grief,

I've noticed; they become careworn effortlessly. I knew I wouldn't let the old house fall down around my ears. But for a long time all was still. Even if we're not flapping about with mates and chicks and all the little wormy things of life, we are still nesting. We are giving ourselves shelter. Our work may be harder, but it is not less loving for being done alone.

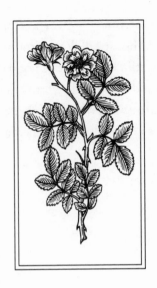

RENOVATION ALERT

I look around the midtown restaurant and see people who look familiar, yet unrecognizable. Face-lifts seem to be on a lot of agendas these days. The results are mixed: some of the surgeries have left behind startling masks, others have been gentler, refreshing. I walk through my neighborhood, and I see the same thing, only this time it's a beloved old house that suddenly appears nakedly new. While I slid into a careless attitude toward my house, preferring (if I want to rationalize my lassitude) to watch it accrue a patina of age (or is that grief?), renovation seemed to be at the top of everyone else's passions.

Our town, on the outskirts of New York City, was developed at the turn of the century, during what I imagine to have been a period of exuberant architectural revival. Handsome Tudors sprang up next to neo-colonials, Victorians next to English cottages, Mediterranean stuccos next to stick-and-shingle piles. A few generations later, many of these houses are victims of benign neglect, if they're lucky. Some wear the flourishes of modernization so popular in the sixties and seventies—sheets of plate glass, pop-top skylights, metal siding, enclosures of anything and everything enclosable: front steps, kitchen stoops, sleeping porches. As it happens, many houses in this town are just now getting their first new owners in thirty or forty years. Empty nesters are selling off real estate whose property taxes no longer make sense. Their children's generation is taking over the mortgages. No sooner do they move in than they roll up their sleeves and call the contractor.

A good thing, too, mostly. I have been living here more than a decade and have watched the gentle decline of many a beautiful building into a sort of torpor, lines dulled, decaying. The wiring shorts out, leaving telltale patches of charred paint. The plumbing dribbles, beams rot, porches sag, gutters jam so that rain and rotten leaves spill a streak of green stain down the walls. Termites chunnel from end to end, roots explode walkways, bees nest in chimneys, plaster crumbles to pillars of dust, slate roofing tiles shatter, and misery trickles in. A contagion of desuetude spreads through our turn-of-the-century neighborhoods.

And then I feel like Rip Van Winkle, finally coming out of a sleep during which I didn't take walks through the town, stopped visiting the friends who were more interested in their relationship with my ex-husband than with me. Divorce is its own sort of disease, I decide, and it carries its own threat of contagion. People shun the divorced woman: she might make you too sad; she might sicken your marriage; she might give your husband ideas. I will never know if these attitudes are figments of my imagination, or real—I can only compare notes with others in my position, and see that we're not too far apart in our perceptions.

So it is with surprise that I come out of hibernation and start walking the streets again, and see that people are coming to the rescue of old buildings. They're able to appreciate the beauty of old bones, recognize the value of old materials, old ways of building. And yet, and yet.

There is such a thing as the overzealous renovation. It is heartbreaking, and it must be bank account–breaking as well. It all happens too fast, everything replaced, repainted, replaned, re-covered, renewed, rethought; gleaming, spanking, screaming new, until it becomes impossible to tell if it was new made to look old or old new. Too much of the past is being erased. There's considerable charm in the slight dishevelments of age; comfort in the smudges of wear; and mystery, allure, in the shadings that only time can grant a house and garden. Life chisels itself into the very floorboards. It seems ill-advised to erase all traces of humanity.

When my son Alex was six, he was asked by his teacher to prepare a science exhibit for the school fair. He went to his

room to think things over—he is a very deliberate person—
and then came down to the kitchen and, full of the quiet
pride so particular to his nature, presented the science project: his beloved Froggie. This was a (once stuffed) scrap of
green (very faded) cotton, rubbed till it felt like silk, bordered
with lace (hanging in tatters), shaped (if you had seen her
many years earlier) like a frog, with big eyes (only one left)
and a dopey (mostly torn-away) grin. My son loved this
thing and wouldn't sleep without her crumpled company
in his little fist, fretting a particular edge of lace between his
fingers. With the true verve of a scientist, which lies in utter
simplicity, Alex announced his plan to glue Froggie to a
board, at the bottom of which he would attach the title of his
project. I was instructed to write on an index card: "The
Effects of Love on a Stuffed Animal."

The same can be said of faces, furniture, houses. We all
fray around the edges. But perhaps it is wiser to keep the redo
to this side of caution. Once the effects of love are undone,
they can never be recovered.

COUCH THERAPY

There was an enormous hole in the living room where the sofa used to be, and I could not fill it no matter how hard I tried. Years went by with the living room looking desolate, or minimalist, depending on my mood, but shop as I might, a good couch was hard to find.

An old leather couch that I had thought, in a wave of nostalgia for a rumpled academic, might be a suitable candidate, ended up in the kitchen. My boys and I spend most of our time hanging out there, with coffee and Pop-Tarts in the

morning; homework, tea, and books in the afternoon; soufflés and cookies in the evening; and general lassitude throughout the weekend. I figured we might as well hang in comfort.
A sofa in the kitchen is a decorating tip worth passing
on. Theo doesn't wake up, mentally, until well after school
has started—as his teachers have been at pains to point out—
so rather than start the day with a struggle, I simply let him
eat breakfast, Roman style, under blankets on the sofa. I get
to indulge him, and he gets to indulge me in my fantasy that
I have gotten him up for school. And what nicer place than
a sofa by the stove for watching a friend prepare dinner or for
sharing a cup of tea while comforting a sister.

It is important that the kitchen sofa be large and soft,
indeed squishy, and sturdy—it will double as a jungle gym—
and boatlike. In fact, we call ours The Boat. It is a fine and
private place for one or two to snuggle in for an afternoon
nap. Its sides and back are high, so it really cradles. Resting
there is like lying in the bottom of a dinghy—an enchanting
thing to do—within the shelter of its sloping sides as you drift
across calm waters. While the kitchen is humming, the living
room goes on looking a little sad. I cannot get my mind
around to what kind of sofa I want in there.

Why is a kitchen sofa so much easier to understand than
one for the living room? Is it the specialness? The formality?
Is that room more demanding? It is not that I do not want to
lie down in the living room. I tend to want to lie down,
most often with a book, wherever I am, and I am prone to
judge the success of other people's houses by how many
places I spot that send out an invitation to rest and dream. But

in the living room I want to be able to lie down and still see out the windows and French doors, or gaze past an arm into the fireplace. And I want also to be able to sit up and talk, and not feel as if I am going to need a forklift to haul me up out of the depths of the furniture. The new enormous sofas I was seeing made me wonder if everyone else might be wearing exercise gear to entertain. Surely no one in a skirt can gracefully negotiate a ledge the size of a Ping-Pong table. That gives you the choice of perching on the edge, if you want to keep your shoes on the floor, or pushing back to lean against a cushion with your feet sticking straight out in front of you like a Barbie doll. Bigger is not better in the couch department.

And that was as far as I could get in my analysis. I simply could not figure out what to do, and I couldn't stop thinking about it. I cannot tell you how many pictures I have seen of decorating projects that were ruined because the scale of the couch was wrong for the room, or the shape was wrong, or the fabric was wrong, or the color was wrong. The couch is the proverbial elephant in the living room, the thing no one wants to talk about even though it is causing lots of trouble. A couch can be like a person you don't want to see anymore who does not get the message. Stubbornly present. Implacable. A constant reminder of an error in judgment. When you make a mistake with a couch, you have made a big mistake. I have had hours of couch therapy (that's therapy about couches, rather than on them) and it turns out my fear of commitment is common. But even though I can pinpoint, unerringly, what is wrong with a couch, I cannot articulate what would be right.

Everywhere I go, every ad I see, every story I look at, I gaze at the sofa and fantasize about what it would be like to be in a liaison with that thing. What would people think when they saw me on the arm of that couch? How would that couch make me feel? Would I look flaky on that West Indian number? Dowdy on that camelback? Is the shoulder on that boxy modern hunk going to be too severe? Is that shabby but charming chintzy thing going to get flabby fast? I see dozens of couches I fall in love with, I scatter snapshots of candidates across my desk, I haunt a couple of close calls, and then, weeks later, I glance at what I thought was the one and think, What was I thinking? All I want is to be held and comforted and protected. All I want is something stylish, yet dependable; relaxed, yet elegant; yielding, yet strong; mature, yet companionable. Is this too much to ask?

Yes, a good couch is hard to find.

LIGHT MY FIRE

If I had to name the one thing in my house that gives me the greatest comfort, I would say it was the fireplace. I have always been the kind of person who likes to sit in front of a fire, but when it came time to mend my soul I *needed* to sit in front of the fire. I spent hours there, gazing dreamily (or wearily or pensively or remorsefully or happily) at the flames. Thinking things over is an activity that is often disdained by the socially hyperactive; it is a "stay-at-home" kind of thing. But how can you trust someone who doesn't crave the peace and quiet of a night at the hearth from time to time? Much as I love a great party, when all of the dancing and drinking and dining and dragging around of the week is done, it feels good simply to rest, and let something else do the burning.

I am lucky to have a few fireplaces in my house; it is one of those things—a wbf, as they say in real estate ads—that should be a necessity but has become a luxury. Everyone should have a place at home for those contemplative moments, whether it is a deep, soft, enveloping armchair, the protective tent of a canopy bed, or a prie-dieu in the dressing room. For many, it's the hearth that lets us burrow into a meditative place.

My father taught me how to build a fire, how to lay the kindling and angle the logs and keep the thing going at a pitch that gives off heat without hysteria. (It will be a mark of generational role reversal that my sons will have learned to build fires from their mother. And they are learning with the same grudging reluctance with which I listened to my father: "What difference does it make, how the logs go on? They're just going to burn." "But it's how they burn that matters." Going right over their heads, for the time being. And yet, my oldest son pays sideways attention, and he lays each successive fire with a little more grace.)

While we were married, my husband made the fires, something, as a New Orleans boy, he wasn't used to doing. It just seemed the sort of thing the man should do, and anyway we didn't sit at the fireplace that often. He was also in charge of the barbecue, and it was understood that the grill was also the man's domain. It came as something of a surprise to me that I was perfectly capable of ordering a cord of wood, stacking it on the back porch, and laying fires to my heart's content—every night, if I wanted to, and I did, for years. It was an even bigger shock when I learned how to start the coals for the grill by myself. There is nothing like taking command of fire for making a person feel powerful, and now I see why men love these jobs and hold on to them long after they have given up all pretense of doing anything else useful around the house.

My father loved to play with the fire, too, and I remember many a goggle-eyed evening when his four children would be lined up at the hearth, flushed from our baths, hot damp skin sending the faint smell of detergent and ironing off our pajamas. Daddy's girls, and our baby prince, watched as he threw magic sticks and pixie dust onto the fire—all made of some highly combustible and probably toxic material that burst into Technicolor flames, putting any acid trip to shame. (This was the kind of thing we did for fun in the early sixties.) These tamer days, I delight my younger son by taking a shovelful of glowing embers from the hearth and melting frankincense on them, sending voluptuously heady clouds of fragrance wafting through the house—tripping smoke alarms, stray cinders burning tiny holes in the carpet. Worth it.

My father ruined his fireplace, as far as I was concerned, during the seventies. Falling prey to anxieties about efficient energy use, as well as some madman's sales pitch, he installed a contraption into the stone surround that sealed off the fireplace with little glass doors. You switched on a noisy fan that was supposed to send the hot air into the room. This is when I learned the wisdom of leaving things alone. But in my father beats the heart of an engineer, the kind of heart that races with delight at any alteration. If he had had his way, we would have had water coursing from out of nowhere down the rock faces of the garden, and docks in the pond that looked like landing strips on naval carriers, and enough lights in the trees to compete with the moon. Such innovations naturally offended my incipient snobbishness about how things should look, but I now see them for the endearing eccentricities they are.

I confess I am not immune to the lure of gadgets either. One of my friends bought me a "Tuscan grill," a contraption of stacking ledges that you fit into the fireplace for cooking. Now I can have picnics in the living room; never mind that the oily stains from grilled radicchio look a little strange on the hearth. It is delightful to cook in a new place, and it calls for a different sort of preparation, simple, more direct. The best fireplace I have ever seen is in a friend's kitchen. It is built up a couple of feet off the floor; there's a wide slab of slate across the front of it, and the kitchen table is in front of that; my friend has a grill built into the fireplace. Whenever I visit I take a seat at the table next to the hearth so I can reach in and snag the crispiest piece of toast, the rarest slice of steak.

There is nothing nicer, when you have houseguests, than to wake early and get a fire going, so your guests are greeted by the crackle of flames when they stumble down to break-fast. A fire in the morning has an altogether different affect—

cheery, merry. A fire draws people in, even teenage boys. Some nights the only way I can get my sons to settle down in the same room with me is to light a fire. It is magical, the way it lulls them into trancelike docility. They become my babies again.

I also have a fireplace in my bedroom, and I love to fall asleep watching orange shadows dance across the ceiling. And of course, with a fireplace comes a mantel, a wonderful place to exercise your creative abilities in the still-life department. I have leaned paintings and photographs on that ledge, and lined up favorite things that change on a monthly basis—rotating the permanent collection, so to speak.

Still the thing that is best about a fire is how much happens while you are leaving it alone. You get it started, and then you watch. You poke, prod, pry a little here and there, but the real activity is in your gaze. Maybe you're watching old letters blaze. Maybe you're just watching the logs. As they are engulfed in flame, all kinds of things burn away. Time drifts; so does pain, heartache. Memories are burnished, thoughts etch into view, hard edges soften. You are in thrall to a consuming beauty, and you choose to feed it, play with it, or let it die. There's a great line from a Leonard Cohen poem (I like it as sung by Emmylou Harris): "Some say love is like smoke, beyond all repair." Where there's smoke . . . Sitting in front of my fire, I realized, after years, how lucky I am to have seen it burn.

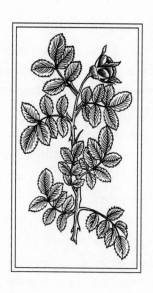

SKI TRIP

Thank God for the children. Somehow mine always knew when to pull me out of my lethargy, and when to indulge me with quiet. Because I had them in my house only half of each week, my sense of the preciousness of our time together was greatly heightened. A strange side benefit to the divorce: my relationship with my sons was dramatically intensified, and for the better. Perhaps, because they were boys, I had stepped back in directing their activities when their father was around; after all, a man would know better what was good for boys. And because their father was home during the day, working out of the house, he had more claim on their time, and was more easily involved in their lives after school. A neat role reversal, one that I had felt proud we had negotiated so deftly, until it began to have a sort of undertow, and I felt subtly, but insistently, shut out of their everyday lives. It was at that level, a level of minor happenstances, banal activities, and silly conversation, that I reconnected with the boys once I was on my own.

No matter how depressed I felt, I could always get going once they were in the house. But they had to jump-start me when it came time to plan the annual winter vacation. None of this staying at home and enjoying the city stuff, Mom. Let's take a trip.

I'm not a baseball mom, or a soccer mom, or a football mom. I was so nearsighted as a child, and this went unnoticed for so many years by anyone in a position to help, that to this day my only reaction to a ball coming at me is to duck. I have been hit in the face too many times. Sports have not, in general, been my thing. But sports are most boys' things, and mine were no exception. I decided we would all learn to ski. I figured: mountains, snow, lifts, exercise, great food, fireplaces, massages, early bedtimes, hot chocolate.

We flew to Colorado one February, and have been going every year since. The trips have been an unparalleled success for us as a family—and I also learned that I could start something that I had thought was life-threatening at my rather advanced age, and have fun with it. We would spend the days on the mountain, and being a competitive enough person, even with my own children, I was determined to keep up with them on any trail. They, being lazy enough, were determined to stay off the terribly bumpy ones marked with black diamonds. So it all worked out. We would be bunked down in our room at the impossibly early hour of nine, having eaten dinner, bathed in the spa pools, and strolled the chic streets. Asleep as soon as the lights were out.

But one night we decided to stay out on the mountain. It was an amazing night. Cold, black bowl of a sky, sharp stars, and a waxing moon. Snow sparkling and ice crunching under our feet, bound into snowshoes, as we made our way up, sucking in the thin air at twelve thousand feet. The branches of the firs around us bowed heavily under the weight of an earlier snowfall. And suddenly, the silent enchantment was broken by the shockingly high-pitched whine of a small boy. . . .

"Mom . . . Mom . . . I'm *hot* . . . I'm *too* hot. Mom. Here. Take my hat."

Another forty or fifty feet up the trail: "Mom. Take my scarf."

Twenty paces later another boy, the larger of the species, joins in: "Here, Mom. My sweater."

So whose idea was it to go on a Moonlight Snowshoe Hike?

Mom, meanwhile, is stuffing all these articles into her pockets, and, when those are full, down the front of her parka. So much for looking attractive on those slopes. Mom now resembles nothing so much as . . . an armoire. A very untidy one, at that. Doors hanging open, every corner hastily crammed, stuff spilling off the shelves. Full, but messy. Or messy but full, is another way to look at it.

You want sturdy? Comfortable? Portable? Enduring? How about biomorphic? Collapsible? Let's talk: Mom as furniture, the ultimate piece of furniture.

I have been them all. Of course, I started my children's lives as their cradle, literally rocking them to sleep as I walked through my pregnant days, and feeling them wake up to kick off the covers and tumble and turn inside me after the cradle stopped rocking as I finally lay down to rest. I have gone on to be their ladder, and their footrest; I'm sure I have even been a table a time or two. I know I have been a chair, holding a child tight in my lap for a cuddle (back in the days when I was allowed such liberties), small head leaning into my shoulder, leg draped heavily over the crook of my arm. La-Z-Boy recliners have nothing on my technique for immobilizing sleepyheads.

Come to think of it, I am the daughter of a vault: one of my mother's admirable traits is that she is entirely discreet and can always be relied on to keep secrets. (A trait that is also frustrating when it comes to learning anything about her mysterious childhood. But a vault is a vault, and there are no teller's hours.) My father is more of a cabinet, brimming to overflowing. And of course it's always fun to think about whose personality tends toward the Baroque, whose is Gothic, and whose is simply, elegantly colonial. I think, as an armoire on that snowy night, I must have looked Rococo.

It's been fun being furniture. It makes you feel like you are never away from home, and puts a new slant on being

home. It could even be said that certain styles of furniture—
particular chairs, say—speak to us, call to us, because they
remind us of their human equivalent in our storehouse of
experiences.

As for the children? They are my hope chests.

TREE HUGGER

As winter draws to a close, my friends and I get busy planning new beds, carving parterres in the snowy ground, outlining imaginary borders with leftover firewood, trying to get a glimpse of how our garden fantasies will shape up. We are ordering plants, buying new tools, stocking up on fertilizer, weighing the virtues of shiny red wheelbarrows—the classic—against the novelty of bright blue ones. But while we're at it with the flowers, I am putting in a word for the trees, and in fact, I have made a decision that trees will be the focus of my garden efforts for the next few years. Trees and walls. Boundaries. Hedges against time.

It is always with great relief that I watch the trees around me begin to leaf out in spring. Relief, partly because I get to tally winter's survivors. I'm anxious to see who has made it through, and in what condition. Pollutants have weakened so many of our trees, making them more prone to blight and virus and other virulent diseases than ever before. But I am also relieved because the leaves begin to provide cover for one of the ghastliest sights in people's yards, along roadsides, and in our parks: the sight of the careless, ignorant, or lazy work of the inept tree pruner. I don't care what they're working on, people with the power to amputate should be licensed. I'm not suggesting years of medical school, but at least some sensitivity training and a course or two in arboreal aesthetics.

I detest the sight of those branches lopped off abruptly at midsection, the pruner not having bothered to take the cut back to the trunk, or worse, simply having decapitated the tree to contain its growth. Stumps yearning heavenward, yet hopelessly thwarted. No respect for the grace or drama in a tree's reach. No consideration for the beauty in the natural tapering of its lines. No twigs left on those stumps to brush the sky and glimmer with the last light of the day, or catch the wind and carry the whole branch into the gentle sway of a dance. I can almost hear the torment and accusation in those stumps—testimony to cruelty, to a rejection of lofty ambition.

Yes, I am a tree hugger. I happily embrace all the nuttiness implied in that phrase, too. I have been a tree hugger since, as a little girl, I climbed into the arms of an old weeping willow and curled up with a book in the welcoming hug of its branches. What pleasure and solace and protection and beauty are to be found in a tree. Such sophisticated engineering in the balance of root and branch, in the resilience of mass against wind. Are trees indeed full of the spirit of the giants who once peopled the earth? Who knows? What matters is that they make us think that way.

My children, who are to be excused because they are still young and have learned only about "life sciences" in school, tell me with great merriment that plants feel no pain because they have no nervous systems. I can't explain to them that it is not a matter of nerve endings, but rather of beginnings— a tree's life affects my system, and I feel pain at our indifference to its integrity.

Why do we do so little to protect our trees? We do not know how it is that the gods walk among us. Only that they slip into our lives quietly, unobtrusively, usually in disguise, and we cross them at our peril. I will never forget a story I read as a child. I have never found a more beautiful distillation of what it means to love, to say nothing of what it means to be a tree. Zeus and Hermes came down from the heavens and, disguised as poor wanderers, entered a village looking for food. They were badly treated by everyone except an elderly couple, Baucis and Philemon, who graciously served them milk and bread and honey. The gods, revealing their true nature—as they always do, eventually, as everyone always does—turned the rest of the village into a lake full of thrashing fish, and granted the couple their one wish: that, when the time came, they might die together so that neither would have to live without the other. Many happy, fruitful years later, when their time did come, Baucis and Philemon planted themselves next to one another and watched each other turn into trees. I imagine they felt their legs burrow and root into the warm soil of late summer, felt their torsos become rigid, canting into some proximity, felt the bark crawl roughly over their bodies, closing in on their hands, their breasts, and, at last, their faces, as they whispered farewell to each other. She became a linden, he an oak. Branches "intertwined together and embraced one another" as Hawthorne tells it in *A Wonder Book for Girls & Boys,* one of my all-time favorite books. "A breeze sprang up and set their intermingled boughs astir . . . and then there was a deep broad murmur in the air . . . the trees both spoke at once . . . as if one were both and both were one, and talking together in the depths of their mutual heart."

It is left to us only to believe. And to cherish. And so I am filled with a need to plant trees, trees that will prosper as I decline, trees that will carry me and my loved ones well into the next century. I don't know if I will ever be so lucky as to find that mutual heart, that steadfast love that can root itself into the soil of an eternity, that will bend my life into another's embrace forever. But I can think of no better sort of hopefulness, and for this alone I will always be grateful for trees.

THE NEW HOUSE

The best way to recover from falling out of love is to fall in love again. I did, with a house by the sea. I can't say it worked like a charm; the fact is I was in love with a man at around the same time, too. But it quickly became clear that, even while the house was in the most decrepit state possible, and the man at the height of his powers, so to speak, it was the house that was going to be around for the long haul. It was the man who fell apart, beyond my repair. So I took on the challenge of bringing the house back to life, and I think at the same time I started to bring myself back to life. It really would not be too much to say, as I can in unguarded moments, that the new house saved me.

It all took me by surprise. In spite of my misgivings I had renewed the rental of our Rhode Island summer house; the bond I felt to this rocky crop of coastline was unfathomable. I simply needed to be in that place. It's funny, what we call home. Some people are lucky enough to feel that home is the place where they were born. Maybe their families go back generations in the same place; maybe their childhoods were so blissful that they never needed to separate who they are, their sense of being themselves, from where they grew up. The rest of us need to find a home, pick a place; some of us have to go so far as to find another family as well, in whose safe embrace we can finally grow into the person we were meant to be.

My ex-husband had always loved the mountains; some people prefer the desert, some are water people. I am, by nature and by upbringing, a water person. My mother and her mother grew up on the coast of North Africa. When the family left in the fifties, my grandmother refused to join them in Paris. She stopped in Nice. "I must look at the sea," she said, "even if it has to be from the wrong side." I cannot think of a time when I didn't live with water nearby—a stream, a lake, an ocean, a fountain, or just an enormous tub. Water lifts my spirits.

My ex-husband took off for the Catskills; I stayed in that patch of New England. But after a couple of summers alone I knew that a rented house was not going to make me happy.

It wasn't mine to alter in any way, to erase old patterns of living. And there were new neighbors—a couple complete with small children—who were always around. They were hovering, anxious people who followed their toddlers all over the garden; and the toddlers followed me everywhere. I was never alone. The last thing I wanted to see, or hear, during the days when I was without my own children, was someone else's family. It was time to leave.

One day, while I was out walking, I noticed a FOR SALE sign stuck in front of a house at the bottom of a secluded private lane. (Naturally I was trespassing, a treasured bad habit.) The house looked strange. A modernist structure built in the fifties, hidden behind several large, prickly old holly trees. The paint was peeling, things were sagging and cracking; the smell of abandonment, which is the smell of infinite generations of mice, wafted all the way across the lawn.

This is not an area that appreciates the modernist aesthetic. Furthermore, the owner of the house had died in it; his ghost was said to haunt it. (Though in my experience ghosts don't go in much for modernism either.) The house had been on the market for years. I walked around the yard, cupped my hands to the picture windows—plate glass!—at the back and peered in at the derelict rooms. Then I sat awhile on the porch, looking out at dozens of mute swans drifting across a marsh pond that I had admired for years.

It took ten minutes. I fell in love. I called my sister, who, bless her heart, is always ready to spend money, the more the merrier. I called the man I loved, who was also very jolly about money. He was the first person I had ever known who encouraged me to be extravagant. And then I called the Realtor.

I had not been house hunting, and I had not been saving money to buy a house. But I did have a severance check from having lost a job; I had been intending to invest in a fund, but why not a house? Why not take the residue of something bad that had happened and turn it into something great? I had discovered the miracle of mortgages when I had had to buy my husband out of his share of our house in New York. I was once again gainfully employed. So I knew I could handle the debt. I put in a low bid. I even gave the owners, and myself, a deadline; in two days, I knew I would have lost my nerve entirely, so I arranged to terminate the offer by then. In two days, I had a new house.

The contractor, whose grandfather had built the original house in the fifties, but whose family had had nothing to do with the second floor that had been piled on in the seventies, told me months later that he would have felt suicidal had he been responsible for the inspection that led me to believe the rehabilitation of the house would be simple, a minor job of cleaning up a few years of neglect. The house was a disaster area. Generations of mice had tunneled into vast colonies of nests and burial mounds in the walls, and had nibbled the very strength from the beams supporting the structure; the joists between the first and second floors were inadequate; the windows were improperly installed and leaked, but perversely would not open; the plastic shower stall was cracked so badly that the wood under it had rotted, and the whole contraption was about to fall through the floor; a heating element mysteriously installed in the ceiling of a bedroom had short-circuited and burned out the tiles; the exterior walls were made of an asbestos sheeting that may have been innovative in the fifties, and was, by the nineties, crumbling and buckling; it went on and on and on. Even the forty-year-old wisteria twisted thickly over an arbor at the back of the house, that had just the previous spring been smothered in fragrant white blooms, gave up and died—after pulling down its rotted wooden support.

I set up shop in the only intact room in the house. It was a guest room that had been built ten years earlier, and even though it, too, leaked in a heavy rain (no flashing over the windows), it was the shelter in which I slept, cooked, ate, and planned and oversaw a renovation that lasted more than a year, though it will never really be done. I was terrified by the amount of work that was needed. But every evening, I sat on the balcony off the second-floor bedroom and gazed out over the pond, and over the sandbar that held the ocean at bay, and over the ocean into the horizon, and I grew stronger.

I realized that I could never have bought a house that was in good shape; once again I needed a needy house. I was deeply happy to give everything I could to this little building. Even the smallest gestures—a pitcher full of jaunty sunflowers, a chime hung in the old maple—made such a difference. When, after many months, I could finally sleep in the big bedroom, I woke every morning with the sunrise spilling gloriously across the floor into my bed. There was the rosy-fingered dawn I had only read about in Homer. If I stayed in bed, I could keep my binoculars glued to my face, watching birds swoop and dive through the meadow and peck around in the branches of a large oak tree. (The feeling of the house was completely different from that of my New York house; in the Rhode Island house you are meant to sit inside and look out—the back of the house is full of windows giving on to the watery views. The New York house turns you inward; there is no view out the windows, except onto tree trunks.) The more energy I poured into the house, the more it came to life, and I came to believe once again in the possibility of shelter.

What is it about the lure of a house on the water? Within an hour of arriving there, no matter what I am leaving behind, I feel a tranquility that I can find nowhere else. The lull of the tides, the silver of the sun on ruffles of waves, the slick, oozy, slimy, gelatinous sea creatures, the long view, the play of the wind, even the subtle threat of the inky depths. To make a home or plant a garden near the water is to choose to live constantly in the presence of a force greater, more mysterious, more beautiful, and more alive than any one of us can ever be—it puts us in our places. How wonderful, then, when we turn our places into a celebration of such brute force. We nestle seaside and are reminded of something important.

One summer many years ago we had taken Alex to the beach for the first time. He was at that toddling age of wanting everything repeated six thousand times, every toss of a ball, every story, every tickle. He ran to the water's edge, planted himself squarely in front of the ocean, folded his arms, and watched a big wave roll in, right to his feet. "Again!" he commanded. And watched with delight at the wave's obedience and his power. Again! Again! Again! So it went all morning. I guess that's it. The ocean doesn't stop. It does not disappoint. It may surge, suck, drown, wreak havoc, but that is its nature and it is always itself, time without end.

When we make our homes and plant our gardens we do it in defiance of endings, with a hopefulness about the future. No matter what surges and collapses in our lives, don't we all keep looking for something that does not end?

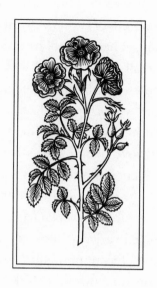

FOR THE BIRDS

The autumn sky is an enormous cerulean dome, rimmed where it meets the sea with the faintest brushwork of clouds; the majestic ceilings in Broadway theaters imitate this dome, and indeed we are in the midst of a great spectacle: migration. My binoculars are by my side at every moment. I wake to the throaty, malignant gossip of crows; I'm transfixed through lunch by the razzle-dazzle of Baltimore orioles; I'm fascinated by the tiny circumlocutions of the midafternoon hummingbirds sipping at the trumpet vine; I have cocktails while hundreds of swallows gyrate for the evening canapés of mosquitoes; herons stalk fish at sunset; doves coo and moan as night falls. My house in Rhode Island was built by avid bird-watchers, and they thought, in siting it, of every possible perch from which to view the birds.

When I moved in, I stopped having most of the lawn mowed. I would love to say it was for ecological—or aesthetic—reasons, but it was really to spare the trouble and expense. I made a few small gestures for the birds and butterflies: I put in a birdbath and planted buddleia to attract beauty of the winged variety. I took great pleasure in the magical appearance of a hummingbird canoodling into the orange trumpet vine that cascades off the pergola. But my efforts were pitiable compared to the enormous attraction I had inadvertently created by letting my lawn go to seed. The meadow of flowers that sprang up a year later became an enormous bird feeder—milkweed, clematis, rambling rose, dock, crown vetch, mullein, clover, thistle, sedges, reeds, and grasses.

Doves, robins, woodcocks, wild turkey, orioles, thrushes, cardinals, finches, mockingbirds, waxwings—all are nibbling, gnawing, stripping, grubbing in the dish that is my backyard. The marsh draws mute swans by the dozens, herons, least terns, piping plovers, gulls, hawks, ibis, ospreys. Letting the field naturalize was the most productive—and effortless—gardening decision I have ever made. I am ceaselessly entertained by the activity of my fleeting ornaments. The birds and the wind are the designers here, transplanting seed from one corner of the meadow to another.

A garden would feel abandoned without birds. So I was very surprised when I learned that the decorating world has a decidedly mixed opinion about them. It is hard to find fabric with a bird pattern in it because it is bad luck. Peacock feathers: an ill omen. I am respectful of superstition, and have my own caprices in that category. But they don't involve birds. Birds are alluring, mysterious, whimsical, gay, and inspiring. I always find the birds and they always find me. I wake to the sound of doves cooing near my bedroom, for they have nested in the arbor over the door. I have my coffee in the company of a pair of cardinals who seem to return to my garden year after year. Hawks circle over my house, osprey dive and soar. Lately it seems as if one of my roles in life is to come to the rescue of wounded or lost or addled birds. All this bird traffic is reassuring to me and I pay careful attention to it. It makes me feel as if some cosmic force is gently reminding me that I have a place in this great stream of life.

Creatures on the wing. You never know where they will take you. I asked a dinner companion recently how he had happened upon his career in Asian art; he is an expert in Chinese porcelains. I expected him to tell me about exotic childhood travels or a love of ancient Chinese literature. Instead, I was startled and charmed by an altogether different connection. As a child growing up in the English countryside, he was crazy about birds, and spent hours, as little boys will, observing and listing and collecting feathers and nests and even (naughtily) eggs. "You could line up fourteen apparently identical eggs and I could tell you the fourteen different kinds of birds whose eggs they were." He had trained himself to observe the subtle gradations in hue, the variations in dappling, the shape and heft and size of the egg. Later on, something about the glazing and crackling—and the fragility and strength—of Chinese porcelains had the same appeal as those eggs. He was taught to appraise the age and make and value of a bowl without turning it over to look at its mark, but by taking its measure in the palm of his hand. That bird-mad boy's imagination took wing, and it carried him into an adult's career.

Decorating is a touchy business. When designers shop, they fondle things, stroking and bunching fabrics, judging whether they meet some perhaps mysterious but strongly felt standard. We all do it—those of us who love things, and who respond to their call, who can't keep our hands off—and bit by bit we carry our treasures home. I guess there's a reason we call it nesting.

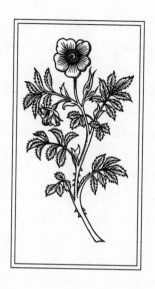

ARMCHAIR LOVE

Have you ever noticed how tenderly companionable a chair can look? It's the one piece of furniture that comes closest to the human form; its shape holds, cradles, cuddles a body—everything we like—and it has arms and legs and feet and a seat and back, and skirts and ruffles, a change of wardrobe to slip into, and sometimes even wings. Something about a chair always brings out the quirkiest facet of a designer's mind; ever since man decided to pick himself up off the floor, the shape of the chair has expressed every sort of whimsy or dignity one could possibly imagine. Chairs can be sexy or noble or cute or cozy or sweet or handsome or elegant or frail. Chairs are the pets of the furniture world; they even creep around a room on their own little paws, or clutch at the carpet with their talons.

I can fall in love with a chair in a heartbeat, and I do, regularly. I now own too many chairs; if my mother were to have the nerve to open my closets (who said it works both ways?), she would find chairs in them. The man who mows my lawn once pointed out that my garden was brimming with pairs of chairs, even though he had seen me only alone. Well, of course a mother needs lots of chairs around for snuggles with her children. But the fact is I get uncomfortable at the sight of a single chair. Chairs are excellent in couples, even in ménages à trois. The garden chairs were there to mark hope—or memory. I knew it was a bad sign that for years my living room was nearly empty. I had kept only one comfortable armchair for reading by the fire, and could not bring myself to find others to join in. I deprived myself of the pleasure of their company. I would bring home candidates—chair candidates, that is—and then give them away, vexed by something incompatible, intangible, perplexing, the moment they came into my house. I was glad when that spell lifted.

Chairs are good for anything and everything; you can eat dinner in a chair or make love in a chair or knit a sweater in a chair. If you're a big reader you pick a chair with an eye to hours of comfortable transport. If you're a fast talker you pick a chair that keeps you light on your seat. One of my favorite chairs is in my bathroom, pulled up near the tub. That chair sits in the expectation that someone will read to me while I soak in fragrant waters. It is enchanting when it happens. Poetry, perhaps a short story, or if I'm lucky for a while, a chapter of a novel. It's the chair where I read to my children when they were young, glancing up from the page now and then to scan the bones of a slender back, a rib cage. What blissful moments.

There is nothing like being read to, except for reading to someone else, or reading with someone else, sitting together in the same room. Many of us learned to read in the lap of a mother or father or doting aunt or bossy big sister. Such warm comfort and such strength and safety in those double sets of arms, the arms of the chair and the arms of love. A safe place from which to watch a new world unfurl.

Eventually, when I had added a few more armchairs to the living room, my sons and I instituted what we call reading room. "Mom, let's have reading room tonight," one of them will say, and it means it is time to light a fire, and curl up together in chairs with our books. It is understood that this is a quiet time, that I am not meant to take advantage of their presence with the usual annoying what-happened-at-school line of questioning. We are hushed, but our sense of togetherness is deep, enveloping.

Chairs are a map of a family. We can read volumes about how people spend time together by where chairs are grouped and how they face one another. It is touching to walk into a well-worn room and see chairs nestled together, in anticipation of another evening with their occupants—or perhaps to mark the place of such a time. I am especially moved when I sit in an old chair and feel the way the cushion has settled, molded over many years with the weight of someone else's habits. It lists toward the reading light, or the little table that always holds a pipe and a cup of steaming tea. There comes a time when no amount of punching and fluffing will relieve a chair of its history.

I have a dear friend who is a devoted reader. I knew the moment I walked into Byron's library that he didn't read alone, either. Two threadbare armchairs sat side by side, each with its own light and its own little table. Ottomans touched their corner tips, like toes. The room was full of books piled everywhere, shelves crammed, and it had an air of surpassing sweetness. I'm a sucker for libraries anyway— one of my favorite movie scenes is in Disney's *Beauty and the Beast,* when the beast woos his beauty with a gift of her very own, four-story-high library, complete with ladders and lights and chairs and tables and books, books, books. Now there's a monster who really understood girls who wear glasses.

I could tell by my strong and nostalgic reaction to visiting Byron's library that I had spent too much time without the company of another reader. Whenever I saw pairs of chairs, I began to fantasize about occupying them, pairs of books, pairs of hearts. Every once in a while I would find myself craving that kind of quiet companionability.

When I last visited my friend's library, he was in the process of packing up and moving out of the apartment. His wife had died, suddenly and unexpectedly. I told him how charming I had always found the little library, and how obvious it was that he had enjoyed it enormously for many years. He confirmed what I had imagined, that one of his favorite ways of spending an evening with his wife had been to read together. I could see them: hours sitting in each other's company, not exchanging a word, the only sound that of pages flicking, the clock chiming, a pipe being tapped out, the flare of a match, the springs of a seat creaking.

"We didn't talk," he remembered. "A long time would go by; we would be completely quiet, each in our own worlds. And yet I was always aware of her presence; I always felt totally connected to her. If she got up from her chair to leave the room, I would feel as though she were leaving in the middle of a talk. I would put my book down and look up, as if she had interrupted a conversation, and say to her, with great surprise, 'Where are you going?'"

SMELL THE ROSES

One summer my younger son informs me that, come September, I will no longer be permitted to walk him to school. Actually, Theo has been gently preparing me for months, dropping big fat hints that he can no longer afford to indulge me in this time together. He knows our morning walks are one of my favorite things, but he is painfully aware that no one else in the fifth grade goes to school with his mother, certainly no one hold hands with his mother or gets a kiss at the corner. Though he has been equally reluctant to say good-bye, as middle school looms a walk with Mom is just out of the question.

It is almost impossible to let go of that little hand. Of course, Theo has had just as much trouble as I have. Those early morning walks—how did they come to mean so much to us? They began, of course, out of necessity. We could have driven to school, but I refused to do that; the school is too close. Eventually I understood that we needed the slow start to the day: the foot-dragging; the whining and complaining (about cold, heat, hunger, sun, rain, nightmares, piano lessons, breakfast); the review of life's small outrages (perpetrated by his brother, his cousins, his friends, his enemies, girls, rabbis, piano teachers).

I came to see that my morning job was to listen, and as there was nothing acceptable to say about Theo's troubles, I began to insert garden instruction into his litany of woes. "I can't believe I have to go to a piano lesson this afternoon," he would begin. "My entire life is ruined and I have scheduling stress." (Apparently the school day now includes classes on how to handle stress, a concept I had never even heard of when I was his age, during which children are taught to put their fingertips together and breathe deeply while they discuss "strategies to avoid riding the conflict escalator.")

"Look, darling, there are Mr. So-and-so's new French tulips," I would reply. "What an amazing shade of orange, and what a great idea, to mix them in with the daffodils. Isn't that beautiful, the way the low morning sun glows through them?" This would be met with a grunt, a new complaint. "Do I really have to take piano lessons? Why can't I take guitar lessons? Why can't I take no lessons?" "And look at that carpet of purple, Theo. That's ajuga, and it's spreading through the lawn." "Sure, Mom." "Those red flowers are camellias, my love. They don't normally grow so well this far north." "Okay, right, whatever, Mom."

And on it goes. Braced for his apathy about the gardens, I plow ahead, partly to counterpoint his aggrieved morning airs and partly out of a belief that if I give him the names of things in the gardens as we walk by, he will eventually care about the things themselves and grow up to be a gardener. So I persist, and he does, too—"I'm doomed, Mom." "Those roses, Theo dear."—down the street, around the corner, up a few blocks, pointing out mosses embedded in cracks in the sidewalks, honeysuckle, irises, lilac, wisteria, peonies, and of course, pines, maples, oaks, sassafras, pears, beeches. We will stop, and I'll poke at a shrub or prod an ant across a mossy knoll, and he'll shiver or groan or sag under the weight of his backpack, and in this way we will delay the inevitable arrival at school until we're more or less ready to let each other go.

Every morning—for years now—my son has responded to my garden enthusiasms with a little attitude of bemusement, as if to say, "There, there, dear, you'll be fine." He knows the drill so well that if I skip the commentary about a particular patch of moss or someone's hedge, he will squeeze my hand and hesitate expectantly at the spot. But he also assures me he will never remember any of the names. "You're wasting your breath, Mom."

Still, I know it won't be lost on him. Many years ago, in

Texas, I heard an old man say to a harried reporter, "Son, you're living life like a clenched fist." I did not want this to be visited upon my son. Who gardens with a clenched fist? Gardens slow things down, relax that death grip with which we grasp the time we are given. I want simply to teach my children to see the roses. One day they will know enough to stop and smell them, too.

THE PIANO

We all have our symptoms. When I get depressed, I stop reading. It is one of the most telling details of my emotional well-being; I know myself by the book. When I am healthy reading is as much a part of everyday life as are sleeping and eating. In the heartbroken years I could not get from one end of a chapter to another, much less navigate an entire novel. I could not concentrate. I could not give myself over to someone else's narrative; I was too mired in my own. Couldn't sustain fantasy. I began to compensate by reading lots of poetry; it was as if that compact wisdom was all I could understand—as if my mind could only grasp briefly at truth, at beauty, at hope, before it folded in on its despair once again.

Doors close, windows open: instead of reading novels, I began to play the piano for hours on end. I had grown up with music, spent hours at the keyboard from the time I was three, though not always voluntarily. My playing had lapsed with motherhood. At the time I figured I was just too busy all day, and too weary in the evening, to practice, what with dinner and bathtime and homework. Even so, I kept my piano with me—a Steinway upright, a graduation gift from my parents—through my days in my first job in New York City to my days as a new bride and a new mother in Austin, Texas, and back again to the Westchester village that we came to call home. Finally, when no one was there to listen, I began to play again. I played and played and played so much that I began to have grandiose ideas about the kind of instrument I needed to express myself, and I decided to buy a grand piano.

I know that many people buy pianos to decorate a room, or to advertise their cultural status, or to place mark an ambition, a hope for the future—someday I will take those piano lessons I have always wanted. None of these things concerned me. I simply wanted a big, powerful instrument, and I wanted to stop sitting with my back to the room. I wanted to entertain myself brilliantly. And I wanted to give myself permission to spend money on something completely unnecessary—or at least not obviously practical—something that would simply give me pleasure. Not land, not a house, not something that would be a sound investment, not something I would share with my family. But something that I was indulging myself in out of my passion for music.

I traveled from one piano store to another, unfolding my dog-eared volumes of Chopin nocturnes and my tattered Beethoven sonatas and Brahms intermezzi and setting them up on the music stands. I am so shy about playing in front of people—even after years of performing in competitions, in front of judges and other musicians—that I had to ask the salesmen to leave the room so that I could concentrate on the sound of the instrument instead of the sound of my pounding heart. After playing dozens and dozens of pianos, I finally found one whose rich, full and yet tender voice thrilled me. The thing is huge, too, way too big for my living room, I'm sure, but its power is intoxicating. I sit in front of it for hours; time unfurls so quickly that often it is two in the morning before I look up from the keyboard. Somehow, putting my hands into the hands of Bach, or Debussy, or Bartok, took me out of my own head. Playing someone else's notes means you must develop compassion for the way that mind worked, and then marry that understanding to the way your own imagination travels. Of course I did not think about any of this when I began to play again. I simply wanted to do it.

The piano became the most important purchase I have ever made in my life, for it brought me full circle back around to my mother, and to the greatest gift she ever gave me: a love of art.

Art is hard work. We want to understand it, and we want to love it, and we want to pass some appreciation on to our children. But it isn't obvious how to do that. We raise them in rooms hung with art. We buy them easels and big pots of paint and watch with anticipation as they "express" themselves. We cherish the clumsy charm in every bit of colored clay that coils through their chubby hands. (In my bedroom I keep a sculpture of a fat bird sitting on a flat barge of a nest, hatching eggs that are not exactly under her, but rather are scattered around, "so she can keep an eye on them, Mom," explained my tiny artist. Every schoolchild's home in this town proudly displays a variant form of Thanksgiving turkey or Halloween pumpkin in clay. This is art that springs from simple, clear, and unreserved hearts, and one of its enormous appeals is that those hearts love us and we love them.)

We drag our children to museums and concert halls. How grateful were my sisters and I, when we were children, for such exposure to art? My mother took us to Lincoln Center once a month for years. We fought about whose turn it was to sit on the aisle. We twisted and squirmed in our seats. We counted the acoustic modules on the ceiling of Avery Fisher Hall. Thirty years later my younger son turns to me during the intermission of a concert and announces, with proud accomplishment in his voice, his tally of the lightbulbs ringing Carnegie Hall. We all listened, and we heard very little. Or so we thought.

My mother gave us piano lessons for many years. Her own musical education was interrupted by the Vichy occupation of Casablanca, the city of her childhood, by curfews, detentions, encampments. Upheaval is not conducive to serious study. Though she was teaching at a conservatory in Boston when she first moved to this country, she soon gave that up as she began to have babies. But she never stopped playing her piano, one she had moved from Casablanca to Cambridge and then on to Connecticut. I fell asleep every night, in my crib, to the sound of her playing Chopin nocturnes. When I play them now, I am awestruck by their strange dissonances, mysterious changes of key left hanging lightly in the air, brilliant passages tossed off, almost asides in a turbulent night drama. I will never know what effect such lullabies could have had on my infant imagination. I do remember, one of my earliest memories, watching the maroon label of an LP (an RCA recording of Rubenstein playing Chopin) spin around and around on the record player, sending out songs that made my mother cry, and I remember sitting in her lap while she was in the strangled reverie of the music, thinking that I wanted to go with her wherever the music was taking her, that I would do anything to keep her with me. I begged for piano lessons, and when I was three years old my mother relented. Washing my hands with great ceremony, she seated me atop a stack of books and spread my little fingers on the keyboard.

By the time she was raising four children, my mother's thwarted ambition had been diverted into a fervent belief that we would simply carry on what had been her promising career. This mission drove her to drive us. She was strict and stubborn and single-minded in her efforts to keep us at the keyboard for hours and hours a day. She always wore a little gold medallion, hanging on a chain around her neck, on which was engraved her motto, "Music and Love." I even think I remember grasping that necklace in a tiny fist while I nursed at her breast . . . but that could be the kind of memory we create in a dream of intimacy. No matter. Music meant the world to her, and she meant to make that our world, too.

The house we lived in when I was a child had a large grid of windows across the back of the living room, overlooking the woods that sloped down to the river. The trees were always filled with birds singing, darting about, pecking at bark, or just sitting and peering cock-eyed. Naturally, I imagined the birds were riveted by my activity in the living room, and I used to entertain us all by playing a few passages at the piano, then getting up and throwing myself into a balletic twirl and leap or two across the room. I would go to the window to see how my audience was responding. Forty years later I have angled my own new piano in the living room so that I can look out the window while I play, and frequently birds will fly up to the house and sit on the trellis, listening, just within my view. I read recently that birds have very bad hearing, but that is such a cruel blow to my vanity that I refuse to believe it. I like the idea that I'm giving the doves and the cardinals pleasure while I play.

I cannot make my children practice for a fraction of an hour. I can't handle their whining resistance. I don't know how my mother put up with ours. As a consequence, one son has run through nearly every instrument in the orchestra; the other quickly lost a good start as a pianist in a hopeless tangle with his teacher. Reproach and recrimination rico-cheted through each lesson until they agreed to fire one another.

There is nothing like music lessons to bring out sheer pigheadedness. It was never clear to me as a child whether we were meant to be controlling the keyboard, or it our lives. One day, devastated with frustration by yet another hour's forced march through miles of Mozart—and certainly sick of the attendant correction and criticism heaped upon her by our mother—one of my sisters gave way to a vengeful rage and, speaking for all overregulated children, took a kitchen knife and carved a four-letter obscenity we had never heard uttered in our home right above the piano's elegant golden logo. Fuck Steinway & Sons. The art of defiance. I have blocked from memory the retaliatory bombardment. I do remember that my mother, sobbing, cleverly recarved the letters, closing up the characters so that they became a ribbon of Mayan-like embellishment, until the wood could be sanded and revarnished.

People who are not used to being with artists—and my mother certainly was an artist, in temperament and training and talent—are shocked by how feelings can escalate around the issue of the hard work that making any kind of art requires: the ruthless solitude of the poet, the relentless appli-cation of the painter, the repetitive diligence of the pianist. Easier to live with the art than with the artist.

And yet, in all that trouble there is something precious. Its value came to me recently as I sat in Carnegie Hall listening to a Rachmaninoff concerto. My mother exposed her children to the language of music, so that as I followed the shifting and shaping voices I could actually understand something of the composer's intention and the musicians' interpretation. She showed us how—and why—to pay attention to art. That gift came to the rescue, as I stumbled through my grief. And it is there to give me pleasure during days of joy. You never know. Making room—rooms—for art in our houses might help us find that place from which to make the art we carry within ourselves.

THAT DAMNED DINING ROOM AGAIN

It's always something. If the dishwasher's finally working, the kitchen drawers start coming unhinged, falling off their tracks and jamming at the exact moment that you need a tablespoon. If the roof is finally repaired, it's the gutters that are backing up, clogged with leaves and sticks and, yes, even baseballs. If the paint job is perfect, it's the carpenter bees that start drilling holes in the trim. If the bathtub is finally draining properly, it's the toilet that won't stop running. It is hard to keep up with a house. Sometimes it is simply overwhelming, and I want to bail out of the whole damn thing.

This time it was the flies that got to me. One day, I noticed a few big, fat, ugly, lazy black flies on the dining room window. I swatted them. A few more appeared in the living room. Got them. This went on, at a slow clip, for a few days, and as I swatted flies I thought, hmmm, the seasons are changing, and then I thought, hmmm, is there a hole in a screen? After a week, and an acceleration of flies, I thought something weird was going on. I put in a call to the local exterminator, got no response, and a day later put in a call to a dozen exterminators. At the rate of thirty or forty flies a day, all fear of becoming poisoned with insecticide had vanished. I would rather that than lose my mind from fly swatting. (Let it be said that I have a few aversions, big ugly flies being one of them.) The boys took turns with the flyswatter, while that was a novelty, and then I was on my own, as still no exterminator had answered my cries for help.

Finally one morning, early, I roused one from his bed with a phone call, and swatting all the while, I explained the problem. He was unimpressed with my crisis; he sounded old and tired and he had heard it all before. "Honey," he said gently, wearily, "I can't help you. Everyone in my company is sick this whole week. There's no one to come to your house. But let me save you some money. You don't need an exterminator. Something has died in your house. Do you have a basement? Do you have chimneys? Do you have an attic? Look in those places. All you need to do is find the dead thing and get rid of it. Then the flies will disappear. They're maggots, by the way."

Oh. He seemed wise in the ways of a house; his advice sounded simple enough and his tone was so matter-of-fact that, all my fear vanished, I blithely set off to check the attic and the basement. I found nothing, of course; when is it ever that easy? I had spent the weekend in front of the fire in the living room, so that was fine, and I wandered into the dining room thinking what a shame it was that I didn't use that room at all, that I had not laid a fire in there the entire winter. The damper was jammed, from disuse I thought—I'm guilty of neglect—and I pushed harder against the lever, a big shove, and then one more time, as hard as I could, and I was in the awkward position of being halfway under the flue when the damper suddenly gave way, spilling out dirt, leaves, nails, debris from the roofing job, and a huge new swarm of flies. Then, to my horror, the bushy black tail of an enormous squirrel, jammed in the flue, came swinging down and brushed against my cheek.

I screamed and screamed. The boys, who were having breakfast, came wheeling in and they screamed, too, and then laughed at me, and then said they had to leave for school before maggots crawled into their clothes.

What to do? I called my father, he wasn't home. I called my sister, she had left for work. I called a friend who would know how to handle such a crisis, imagining that he might actually get in his truck and drive two (okay, three) hours from nearby Rhode Island to help me. What is my problem? I felt helpless, choking with disgust and insecticide, still feeling the squirrel on my face and listening to the angry buzz of more maggots dying. I stood at the dining room window, watching the trickle of men from the neighborhood who were walking to the train, thinking, where is the man who would help me here, surely there's one out there? Could I just nab one off the street? It's no wonder that women fall in love with their handymen, or have fantasies of running away with them. I would, too, if there were a man handy.

Someone finally suggested that I call a chimney cleaner. I did, and then I left for the office, and while I was away everything was disposed of and cleaned up. The buzzing stopped. Now my chimneys have horrible steel caps on them, as if they've been to the orthodontist, and of course I didn't save any money at all but spent a small fortune. It will be weeks and endless rounds of phone calls and haggling before the caps get taken off and a simple screen is screwed into place.

Days later, still whimpering at the death that fell into my fireplace, I told a friend, skilled in the art of feng shui, how overwhelmed I had felt by not being able to handle yet another thing gone wrong in the house. "It never ends," I complained. "It seems like constant breakdown."

"Yes," he agreed. "Isn't that the amazing thing about houses? They're so alive."

SACRED ORDINARY

One way that I marked the passage out of pain was in my relations to things, to simple household objects. When I was suffering, everything seemed dead, lifeless. I could no longer see or feel the animating spirit of even a beloved object. Of course my children would protest that things are, by definition, lifeless; I can hear their nascent scientific umbrage: "Mom, things don't have lives. They don't have nerves or blood. You probably still think love comes from your heart, right, Mom? It doesn't. Love comes from your brain. Your heart pumps blood."

What are they teaching these children in school? I remind them of Valentines—we say I love you and we are not drawing arrows through brain stems, are we? I remind them of that funny feeling near their stomachs, not in their hair. To no avail. I remind them that for millennia we have said my heart is breaking, not my brain is breaking. We have rehearsed this discussion so many times that the lines are scripted, but every time it makes them very merry. I am supposed to insist on the heart's power, and on the spirit of the things around us. I have come to believe that they find the possibility of unreasonable answers reassuring.

But the kids think I'm finally cracking up early one day when I tell them to bundle up and get in the car. We have to drive to the consignment shop because something there is calling me to come and buy it. Far from cracking up, I am waking up. When we get there I find two of the most gorgeous candlesticks I have ever seen, carved of a red agate, trimmed with bronze fashioned into dragon tails and mermaid heads that wrap themselves around the base. I'm triumphant. The boys' eyes are rolling in their little heads. But they are indulgent, I buy them treats, too, and when we get home they move the candlesticks around from the dining room table to the kitchen sideboard to my bedside table and then, finally, to the living room mantel, where they decide, in spite of themselves, that the candlesticks are happy.

And I am happy. Because even though, after several years of being on my own, and still taking to my bed on occasion, overwhelmed, I feel alive again. Attuned to the lives around me. I see beauty, again, and I feel the spirit pulsing in the things of everyday life.

It is a powerful feeling, to be able to render an ordinary object sacred, to imbue it with so much meaning and memory that it is animated by your tender gaze. I had several boxes in the attic full of things I had put away years earlier, things that had once lived on my nightstand. Those objects had calmed and comforted me, before they came to remind me of a life once shared. I was ready to see them again. It was not lost on me that there were still days when I didn't want to crawl out from under the covers. But at least I wanted to change the view from my mattress; I reckoned this an improvement in my outlook, even if taken in measures that seemed faintly ridiculous.

My bedside table became again my little altar to the gods and goddesses who protect and nourish and guide and punish. I covered it with offerings of love, and arranged and rearranged them with a fetishistic superstition that would warm the hearts of the ancients. (One of my sons is the same way. Since he was a toddler he has been organizing, on his night table, displays of matchbox cars, buttons, bits of glass, tiny dinosaurs. Is this genetic? Are we coded for ways of comforting ourselves?)

Buddhas of ivory and bronze, crosses of ebony and mosaic, pillars of candles, carved saints, *figas,* bits of sea glass, smooth beach pebbles, a scrolled and curlicued hand of Fatima—this last probably the thing I am most superstitious about—a legacy from my mother's Moroccan childhood. (The day each of my newborn sons came home from the hospital she slipped a little hand under the mattress in the crib: to protect them from the evil eye, she explained. Leave it there, don't touch it. I did as told.) I propped against the wall a beautiful lithograph by an artist named Alan Magee, a picture of a mottled gray stone simply floating in white space. It had been pulled out of a private bin by a friendly art dealer who wisely intuited that the sight of such durable, commonplace beauty would do me good.

Every night as a little girl, I greeted bedtime, like millions of other American children, with the recitation of a popular prayer: "Now I lay me down to sleep / I pray the Lord my soul to keep / If I should die before I wake / I pray the Lord my soul to take." The terrifying threat so innocuously implied in the verse is engraved in my heart. Perhaps I have created little altars to propitiate Anyone who might get Any Ideas about ripping me untimely from the bed. "Turn around," I wanted my night table to say. "Go find another child to take away." I suppose the protection of the table mattered even more to me as a woman who was as often as not going to bed not sure whether she wanted to wake up again. The things I placed around my bed were talismans against that kind of despair. It is hard to know, sometimes, when or why ordinary objects take root in our lives. But sometimes we're lucky enough to see it happen right before our eyes.

One weekend I was invited to the home of some friends for a bris and naming ceremony for their newborn twins. As the moyel prepared the living room for the ritual, I noticed that David had placed his favorite armchair center stage. I had been with him months earlier in the showroom when its strong, handsome lines had caught his attention. The moyel draped a deep purple silken cloth over the back of the chair, and each tiny child in turn was laid in a pillow on the seat. The gracefully swooping arms embraced each baby as prayers and blessings were chanted, portraits snapped. Babies wailed and sympathetic, joyous tears streamed from generations of family and friends. I hope tears stained the chair.

As I watched, I knew that the chair would too soon hold a child and David as he read aloud, David lecturing a child at his knees about a bad report card, David brooding about a teenager's missed curfew, David waiting for news of safe passage into this world for his children's children. . . . I thought about the armchair in which I had nursed my babies, because its arms were so supportive. I thought about the armchair in which I read by the fire, because its back was so strong and its seat so deep and cushy. I thought about the armchair my father used to sit in, while I played the piano; he would gently doze off, and wake with a start and a bit of applause when the piano was silent.

A few weeks later, I celebrated my birthday with my boys. My older son Alex had written a beautiful poem thanking me for all I had given him. And, he emphasized, it rhymed. Theo handed me a lumpy package, something balled up in Kleenex tied with a bit of string. Alex couldn't resist a snort of derision but I cut him off. I can't wrap things either, and who cares?

"It gets worse, Mom," said Alex. "Wait till you hear where he found your present."

Theo was defiant. "Open it." I pulled away shreds of tissue to find a little candleholder. Brightly painted ceramic pansies surrounded the little cup; it was stained and a few petals were broken off, but the thing still had a jaunty spirit.

"Theo, thank you," I said. "This is lovely, and unusual, and it is useful, too."

"He found it in the trash, Mom," said his older brother. "In *someone else's* trash."

Theo drew himself up with great dignity. "I was walking to school on trash day, Mom, and I saw it in someone's pile down the street. They didn't want it anymore, but I thought it was beautiful and you would like it. So I hid it in the woods for the day, and brought it home after school and cleaned it up for you."

He closed his defense with a twinkle in his eye.

"It called to me, Mom."

REPAIRS NEVER END

The bumper sticker on the truck reads: We can fix anything except a broken heart and the crack of dawn.

That's more than I can fix. And for that reason, I love having men around the house. Men with tools. Men who know about the furnace, and the shingles, and the gutters, and the drainpipes, and the sump pump. I don't know about any of these things. I don't understand any of the creatures living in my basement, with their strangled clicks and gurgles, their fastidious ticking through the night, their hulking mass. I don't like the passive-aggressive nature of all that equipment, prone to whining, jangling breakdowns for no apparent reason. I don't like the looks of those thick wires snaking across the ceiling and disappearing to do God knows what in the walls. I don't like the atmosphere down there, either; how can a place that's cool and clammy be full of monsters that are burning with trouble? The only things I like to visit in my basement are the wine bottles.

Okay, I know it doesn't have to be men you turn to for understanding. I know that somewhere in the world there are women plumbers. Just like there are women contractors and women electricians. Just not in my town. I know, too, that I have been behaving like the classically ditsy girl who doesn't get a thing about her house. And I'm sick of it.

Why didn't they teach us anything useful, in all those hours of home economics classes I took in high school? Why don't I know a Phillips head from whatever? A hammer from a mallet? A wrench from . . . whatever, again? My father has tried, on several occasions, to set matters right. He bought me a beautiful set of tools when we moved into our house; and I even bought a beautiful shiny red toolbox to put everything in, thinking, with typical screwball logic, that if I have a nice box in which to put things, I'll actually take them out and use them. I haven't used them, but somehow, one by one, every screwdriver, wrench, and drill bit has slowly but surely gone missing.

In my childhood home, my father had built a handsome, sturdy workbench in his workshop. That he even had a workshop was admirable in itself, and it was a place forbidden to us unless we were with him. The workshop was endlessly fascinating, especially as, over the years, things were accumulated, piled, sorted, arranged, and abandoned. Eventually the workshop looked like the sort of place an archaeologist might enjoy. But when I was young, the workshop was pristine, and every dangerous-looking thing hung smartly in its proper place.

My father knew how to build things. He built furniture for us—my first headboard, with a shelf to hold books, a chest for my blocks, a dollhouse. He even built a room for my grandmother when she came from Morocco to live with us. He carved the space out of our playroom; it looked as if he were outlining it when the studs went up, and then he pulled the wiring through the walls, and hammered on the Sheetrock. The whole contraption was marvelous, and it was during its construction that I suddenly understood that rooms didn't simply happen to exist; they were built. Someone decided about them. You had a lot of choice about where they went and how large or cozy they were and what they looked like.

Nothing ever stayed broken for long in my childhood home; even things that weren't broken were constantly being enhanced, upgraded, bettered. My father loved nothing more than coming home from a day of surgery and tinkering with wood and nails and such; I was always on hand to assist. So you would think I would have picked up some helpful information.

Instead, I picked up a dependency on people who know

how to fix things. And some of them have been utterly trust-worthy. Others have been scoundrels, or worse, villains, for there is nothing more awful than being taken advantage of at home. Of course men are prey to this as well as women, and yet somehow I can't help feeling that women are a little more vulnerable; it is assumed, and usually correctly, that the female client knows absolutely nothing about the problem that needs fixing and will pay anything to make it go away. I am clearly a case in point.

I have a friend who, even years after its completion, could not talk about building her new house without cry-ing, her experience with the contractor had been so devas-tating. I stood in my own newly renovated kitchen one day and watched rain drip from the ceiling. The roofer who finally showed up to fix what I thought was a leak pointed out that the doorsill in a room above the kitchen had been installed backward, so naturally rain was flowing into the house. It's been ten years since the renovation, and prob-lems still crop up. Then there was the new furnace, which lasted a mere seven years of its lifetime guarantee (a con-cept, by the way, that is sheer fiction, lifetime being a self-defining characteristic—if it is broken, its lifetime has ended), installed incorrectly by a plumber who had the nerve to offer a discount on the installation of the next one. So I started all over again with another plumber. Each new contract I sign is an act of faith, and it is signed with a prayer that the work will be done, and done well, that ill will won't haunt the premises.

I guess there's no way to guarantee that you won't be at the mercy of the repair trucks. But hey! Those guys don't know everything. I've noticed that the crack of dawn fixes itself, each and every day.

And I am learning how to mend a broken heart.

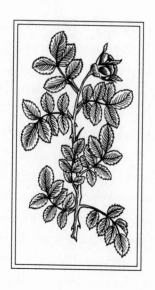

PATCHWORK

Bundled up against a bitter December cold, I set out for a long walk in the Rhode Island countryside. I am fascinated by the lives of the gardens—in every season—on this rocky coast. There is only one smoking chimney on my lane; all the other houses are closed up until the summer. Thus I am silently granted leave to cut through yards and across pastures, climb over stone walls, and find the shortest path to the sea. Along the way I inspect all the gardens, down, too, for the winter. I don't care what anyone says, dormant gardens are not, as a rule, beautiful. Yes, there's the occasional blush of color to admire—the crimson hue of a peculiar bark, say, or one late bloom arrested at the tip of a gangly stem, the carve of beds in the lawn, brought into relief by a dusting of frost. But mostly it's a dismal sight.

Vines curl and shrivel mid-reach; hosta beds wilt and mound like salad left overnight; rose stalks wither cronishly, nothing left to soften thorny edges. Dozens of little name tags poke up out of their earthen beds like tiny tombstones. It takes an act of will to imagine what life they once marked. And it is in winter beds that one finds the remnants of summer play—the lost sneaker, the stray ball, the misplaced trowel, now rusting, half buried in the dirt. Winter gardens are full of ghosts and memories; as T. S. Eliot says in *Four Quartets,* filled with "the hidden laughter of children in the foliage." Perhaps that is really the gift of the winter garden. Rather than being a delight for the eye, it offers a chance to listen for the voices.

My own garden in Rhode Island does not look like much in the winter; I did not have enough ambition to give it a strong structure, and I rationalize my laziness by sweeping to the view of the marsh, and explaining that nothing could compete with that, so a natural look is appropriate. But in the summer my garden is a regular chorus, probably in danger of becoming a musical comedy. There's the Lover's Bed: so-named partly because a kind man helped me carve it out of the lawn (my first adult experience of gardening with someone I loved, and whose happy hours taught me much about how once-solitary pleasures can be enhanced by glad-hearted company). The Lover's Bed is the home of Miss Depressa, a weird, blue-green dwarf hysteric who grows along the ground, never quite touching down. She's a fainter, a lonely one. She is accompanied in her drama by a handsome, sturdy dwarf fir who grandly sports one—only one, and I nearly slapped the hand of a greedy child who once tried to snap it off—outsize pinecone.

There's Gary's Wall, named for my old friend who rolled up his sleeves one day and, in time-honored farmer style, spent an afternoon artfully piling rocks into a new barrier at the edge of the lawn. (There's the kind of houseguest we love; he doesn't ask what can be done, just sees a need and takes care of it.)

There's the Path of Last Legs that meanders down to the canoe lying on its side, waiting to be put into the marsh pond. That path had once cut straight across the lawn from the back door to the water. When I got rid of the lawn—or let it go to pasture—I got rid of the path as well. I decided I wanted the trip to the pond to take a little longer, and the path to be more subtle, so I sent it off in the opposite direction to the side of the yard, to curve around and pay respects to a couple of old black pines on their last legs. This peninsula used to be covered with black pine, and they are almost completely gone, victim of the kind of blight that wipes out an entire neighborhood of gardens. It is a bad idea to plant too much of one thing.

There's the Guest Bed, created in front of the guest room for my favorite visitors, who wanted something curtaining "their" window; I gave them thick sprays of ornamental grasses. But I must have taken a minimalist approach with this bed, for everyone who sees it wants to add something. My neighbor David offers what's left from the thinning of his beds, beds his mother helped him put in, with things from her own garden next door, years ago. I accept happily. Another friend comes to visit with an armful of daylilies, and what's more, he plants them for me, in the Guest Bed, in the Lover's Bed, along the Path of Last Legs. He taught me to snip off a couple of blooms in the morning, and float them in a bowl of water, so I could see them on my desk. (I add to every bouquet a couple of sprigs of the mint that is taking over the Lover's Bed; it smells quite chipper indoors.) Years later, even though I haven't seen him, his lilies have returned again and again, their yolky faces a sunny reminder of his caring and generous heart. And so I hear the voices of all who accompany me as I carve my patchwork into this seacoast.

My grandmother in Kentucky used to make dresses for all her grandchildren. I remember she would lie me down on the floor, perfectly still, on brown paper—grocery bags cut open and flattened—so that she could trace a pattern around my little body. I would watch over her shoulder as she transferred the pattern to fabric; the scraps would go into a quilting bag. Nothing would be thrown out; that would be unthinkable. My boys and I, and my sisters and brother and cousins, sleep under quilts patched together over the years by my grandmother, and her mother, and then her daughters. Sometimes I finger the tiny squares and imagine the dress or shirt someone wore, someone I knew and loved. So it is, looking out over our gardens. Not a seed wasted. Not a plant without a memory.

The Rhode Island gardens I am especially drawn to tend to have a muscular design that makes them seem a permanent part of the landscape. This is what gives them great winter presence, in spite of their empty beds. The bulwarks built against the brutal elements of this climate become the structure that survives every season. These gardens were created in a place pounded by hurricanes, tidal surges, cold winds, salt spray, heavy fog, and those killing freezes that come tragically late in spring, after buds have begun their tender swelling and are once again vulnerable to the cold.

The ocean is large and unquiet, and it meets a land of granite cliffs. The beaches are stony, fields are full of boulders, many of them as big as houses, some cleft in two by imponderable forces. Anyone who gardens in the face of all this is stubborn and faithful and optimistic. Since colonial days, countless English-style flower beds have come and gone without leaving a trace, succumbing to casual disregard or the blunt trauma of a nor'easter.

Many of the gardens here grew out of a New England reverence for dry walls. No good Yankee garden would be without one. A friend presides over a property ringed with magnificent, deep flower beds, but the most endearing feature of his garden is a small semicircular bed carved out of the lawn and close enough to the house to be enjoyed from the comfort of a wing chair near the parlor window. The flowers are massed within the curve of a beautiful, low stone wall. The wall was built for my friend's grandmother, whose husband had offered her, for their anniversary, her choice of two gifts: a string of pearls or a new stone wall. Being a woman of Yankee rectitude, she naturally chose the wall. And the bed became known to the family, down the years, as the String of Pearls. Friends gather at the String for sunset cocktails or morning coffee. The plants within its clasp may change from year to year, but the String of Pearls stands unbroken.

And so a garden endures. On my winter bicycle trips, I chance now and then on the occasional ghost of a garden. Even in wild abandon it has a skeletal beauty. The bones, indeed, are the last to go. There are some things we can never really possess; we simply take our brief turn at tending them.

BERMUDA TRIANGLE

There is nothing tame about a kitchen. I'll accept that it is the heart of the house, as everyone likes to say, but only with the proviso that it is a wild heart that is beating there. The heat we're always hearing about—"If you can't stand the heat . . ."—isn't the heat of a Viking range. What's coming from the kitchen is the heat of emotional experience, and there's no getting out.

Remember when, not long ago, women wanted to be liberated from the kitchen? Now that more men are cooking, and cooking has been elevated to a competitive sport (if not an artistic endeavor or a religious experience), that has changed. But once upon a time, the kitchen was where you left your mother when you went off to school and where you found her again at the end of your day. Time was you didn't want to get stuck there, and now you can't find enough time to be there. The kitchen was the place for reunion, for planning, for messages, for reminders, for budgeting, the place where a family tore the passing days off the calendar. It is still the town hall of the house, even if our patterns of gathering are different. Think of how weekends can revolve around the kitchen, how parties drift in and out of it, and how many important conversations happen there.

For countless families, the kitchen is the forum for impassioned argument, or worse. You notice how often it's really one person's kitchen—even if two or more use it? Buried beneath the words of any kitchen fight is that dance to take control of the magic triangle—the pathway from stove to refrigerator to sink—to maneuver into position, like a sailboat in a regatta or a squash player on the court, and to command what becomes an unholy vortex. What a terrifying place to fight, with all those weapons lying about. But I can see how all the activity of sorting or scrambling or chopping or beating lays a nice rhythmic line of counterpoint to the words, forcing all the players to pause and take the measure of something beyond the conversation. Allow to cool. If you are lucky, some delicious alchemy takes away the sting of tearful talk.

And yes, there is that comfort in food. When I was a

teenager, my strict mother gave me permission to enroll in a bread-baking course being held in the middle of a school day at a nearby shopping strip. It was an act of unprecedented leniency; I guess it was the seventies, too. But I will never find a better therapy than kneading and punching dough and watching it rise again. The yeastiness of fun. My eating habits are disgraceful, but I rigorously defend the virtue of a chocolate soufflé for dinner. (Protein, and a nice little sugar lift at the end of the day—why bother with the rest of the meal? This is a big improvement over my other favorite meal, a bottle of Guinness in front of the fire.) And if it is sleeplessly late and the house feels dark and too quiet and hollow, nothing beats a bowl of Cream of Wheat, accompanied by the friendly hum of the refrigerator. The kitchen is a nice place to be lonely.

If you can navigate the Bermuda Triangle, a kitchen is also a great room for company. I'm suspicious, now, of those who must always cook alone. There's nothing merrier—or sweeter, or sexier—than that domestic minuet around a recipe. I'm no longer embarrassed to admit that up until fairly recently, I thought the flashing neon signs on the fleshpots of Forty-second Street in New York City said "Hot! Hot! Hot! Live! [rhymes with 'give'] Live! Live!" Okay, now I know that "Live!" rhymes with "Dive!" But I like it better the wrong way; it's the right idea. So let's dish out saucy praise for that place of crazy salads, spicy endearments, whispering soufflés, sweetmeats, tender loins, and sticky fingers. That whirring, blending, mixed-up, soul-stirring, juice-dripping, hot-hearted room.

BED RIDDANCE

Some bad months, and then some great months, piling up into years. That's how healing works its way in. Just when I would feel I was pulling out of the tunnel of sadness, I would find myself there once again, often for no discernible reason. I couldn't sleep. Sleeplessness wasn't so unusual, actually, but this time it wasn't because I was mad at my mother, or anxious about a child, or missing someone's company, or worried about an early morning flight. It was because my bed was bugging me. I realized as I tossed and turned that I was beginning to hate my bed. I had bought it because we had never owned one as a married couple, never gotten beyond the mattress and box on a metal frame. It seemed important, very important, as I was trying to pull together the decimated house, that I put real furniture in the bedroom, and create a place in which to rest while the broken bones of my life knitted themselves. As anyone could have warned me, I hopped right into the wrong bed.

Fell in love with it. Had to have it. Even though it was wickedly expensive, perhaps ungainly, or a little overpowering, if not downright decadent. Maybe not; maybe this is just how things look when the burnish of new love has worn off. Sometimes you skip the patina stage.

Anyway, the bed had served me just fine. I had the right impulse with the whole bedroom thing. It was a refuge, and it even became a place of happiness from time to time. But inexplicably, the bed had begun to bother me. I can't say when this started. It wasn't that the bed had changed; it was still dark and tall and handsome. It was me, somehow, or it was something hiding under the bed.

And that raised the whole ugly issue of giving yourself permission to redecorate, which I was of a mind, finally, to do. How could I justify spending money on another bed? Do I count the nights I spent in this one, and divide that number into the ungodly price (including tax and delivery) to see if I've amortized the whole thing efficiently enough? What do you do with an old bed anyway? It's awfully big, hard to give away. And then again, not big enough for many; it isn't king-size, to say nothing of California-size. My sister wouldn't take it; she sleeps on a bed the size of an island, or a cloud. The consignment shop? One of my sons? But do I want to give either one a bed big enough to fit a girlfriend someday? Forget it!

What kind of split personality do I have, anyway, that I can want one kind of bed so badly and then, after a mere few years, want exactly the opposite kind? What kind of Penelope would I have made? When her long-lost Odysseus finally returns, after twenty war-torn years, the reason she comes to believe that the stranger before her is indeed her beloved husband is that Odysseus can describe, in perfect, eccentric detail, the marriage bed he had built for them, using an ancient olive tree, still rooted in the ground, as one of the bedposts. I probably would have sawed the whole thing down years earlier, in the name of redecorating, or to change the karma, or to make room for a bigger loom. But that's another story.

Luckily, the bed I can't bear any longer is of the shallow-root variety. Even though I started out thinking it would be one of those things that would last eternally, I have learned to admit my mistakes with a little more speed. I know now, instead, that it will take me an eternity to find the right one. But I'm ready to start looking again. Maybe I'll try the Zen thing for a while, and experience the Bed of No Bed. (Not that the Sleep of No Sleep has been so marvelous.) Maybe the point is that I've come to believe in getting rid of the things that trouble your sleep.

Well, not quite. I would like to keep my mother forever.

MOTHER'S DAY

I can never tell why, or when, I am going to move into one of those states in which I cannot stop worrying. Tonight I am exhausted. I have been on too many airplanes in the last few days. My mother is about to go into surgery, and she begins the old familiar litany when I call from an airport to wish her luck. Our conversation is punctuated with announcements of arrivals, delays, cancellations, departures. "If anything happens," she begins, "I want you to know—" I cut her off. I cannot listen, I have heard it so many times throughout my childhood. Every time she left the house she anticipated a car crash, a plane crash, a train crash, loss of life, which for me meant loss of love. Of course I believe what she tells me; the chance that I will lose her forever is much greater than the chance that she will take care of me forever. Naturally, this weekend, I think my mother will die. Is this the root of another anxiety that takes hold of me tonight, that my own children will be torn from me?

I slide into one of those states in which everything breaks my heart. I cannot bear to read the newspaper; one disaster after another comes to life before my eyes. Today it is the teenaged boys in Israel who skipped school to go hiking in the hills. They are found in a cave, heads bashed in with rocks, lying in pools of their own blood. I am racked with pain for all the world's parents. Everyone's anguish is mine, and then I start to think that something awful will happen to the babies I love so deeply. I am not alone in this affliction. So many parents I know are overcome, from time to time, with anticipation of disaster, of unrelenting grief. We rehearse for it. We pray that we, that ours, will be spared. We lie awake, imagining the worst, we wait at the door, we sit dumbly at our desks, we worry, we give ourselves terrors. We obsess about other parents' tragedies. We fear for our own fierce love.

I have flown into Rhode Island from a business trip in Chicago; I need to see if some flood damage to my house has been repaired. I would not be with my children this evening under any circumstance—it is a day when they are meant to be in their father's care—but I'm feeling the pain of their absence anyway, as sharply as if the divorce had just begun, as if I hadn't been on this schedule of separation and reunion for years. I will never adjust any more than I have, which at times feels as if it is minimally, functionally, at best. I am driving toward the sea; I stop at a convenience store for bottles of water and milk, and even though it is dinnertime I can't think of what I want to eat. I can only think of the Palestinian infant shot to death in his mother's arms, as she nursed him at her breast in her garden, basking in the morning sun. As I head past town I wonder if I should stop at the so-called (by my children) Liquid Store to buy a bottle of wine, and I wonder if I'm becoming an alcoholic because I want that Chardonnay in my glass at dusk. I decide I can pass it up if I want to, and I don't want to, so I stop, but I end up buying only a half bottle of something wretched just to make a point. I cannot believe I am even having this discussion with myself.

So is it guilt that brings on the anxiety that something will happen to the children, guilt that I'm alone in the country with a glass of wine? Guilt that I have been crisscrossing airports, doing my job? My children will be snatched from me in divine retribution for my having upset the natural order of things by not staying married, not staying home, not driving car pools, not working hard enough, not being good enough.

Is it sorrow, that I'm alone, that I don't have anyone with me, that brings on the fears? There is no one here to comfort me, my friends are far away. I have chosen, over and over, to live alone; I crave solitude. Yet I also crave the company of love. Tonight all I feel is loneliness.

Guilt. Hormones. Fear. Sensitivity. Whatever it is that visits me and leaves me in a panic of loss, can never be named. Perhaps it is inextricably linked with having borne infants into this world in the first place. They are not the only ones left helpless once the umbilical cord is severed, once the placenta lies blue, bloody, wilting in the surgeon's pan. The connection is broken. Putting the baby to your breast, miraculous though that is, is a mere approximation of the life-giving force you once had, for you know that if he won't suckle, help is close to hand. There are substitutes for your vital juices. You can keep a vigil by his crib, cupping your cool palm across his forehead, brushing back wisps of hair, tucking in a sheet. But you are no longer the monitor of his tiny pulse, knowing his heart beats as one with your own. You can no longer register every kick, twist, stretch, or hiccup, as he curls in his watery domain just under your lungs.

He is born. He is on his own. And so are you.

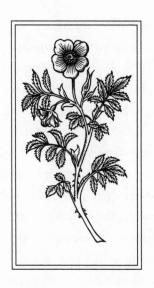

WHAT'S MISSING

One evening my aunt in Kentucky confided that she was worried about her nephew's not having a place to live. He had just lost a lease, and graduate housing in New York City was almost impossible to find. I immediately invited him to live with me while he searched for an apartment. I was rattling around in the house; I still hadn't recaptured all the space left empty on the third floor, so my cousin would have plenty of room. And I thought it would be good for the boys to have another boy in the house, an older role model who was young enough to play with them.

A few weeks became months, and we had a wonderful time; my sons and I loved his company—he is the kind of delightful person who is always going to be much younger than his years. He was constantly offering to do things around the house, unlike my own children, but I could never think of anything minor that needed to be done. (Of course, you never can when someone's there to help. It's only when you're alone that those lists unfurl into the night—doors off their hinges, dimmer switches blown, books looking for shelf space.) Besides, there was a little too much of the medieval scholar about my cousin for me to be able to imagine what he might do with a hammer.

But one fine summer day I relented and asked for help cleaning out an overgrown bed in the garden. I was pleased that I had shaken off some of my lethargy and was finally in the mood to pull on the garden gloves, and thought the company out there would be nice. He performed the simple weeding job meticulously—except that in his zeal he hacked away a clematis vine that for ten years I had coaxed and coddled across the face of an ugly concrete retaining wall. I am mortified to admit that I did not do a very good job with the retaining wall of my frustration at his carelessness—or ignorance—and rather than a gracious and lighthearted shrug, I burst into copious tears. Poor dear, I'm sure he had no idea what to make of a person who could be so emotional about a vine.

I have no idea what to make of people whose hearts *don't* break in the garden. I have wept profusely, unashamedly, over a number of garden tragedies: the hydrangea who strangled herself with her own roots; the noble maple split in half by lightning; the fifty-year-old wisteria gnawed to death by a monstrous vole. The worst disaster was years earlier, when a huge limb of an American dogwood was lopped off by a "landscape artist" who took it upon herself to "clean things up and let some light into the yard so the grass could grow." I would have traded every blade of grass in the lawn for the branch that arced gracefully down to the ground, covered at the start of spring in a thick, beautiful fan of white flowers. I sobbed, ranted, and raved for a week. I wanted to have the woman arrested. I wanted her license revoked. I wanted revenge. And every spring, when what's left of the tree is in a halo of blossoms, the wound left behind by the branch begins to ooze, and a strange thick liquid runs down the trunk, as if the tree were weeping, too. The stigmata of a dogwood.

I will always see that limb when I look at that tree. And I will always see that clematis spilling over my kitchen wall (and of course it is growing back, more unruly than ever). We have all visited gardens only to hear the hostess, pointing haplessly, vaguely, to an empty patch of grass, say feebly, "That was the rose garden . . . and those rhododendrons used to be nine feet tall until the hurricane of . . . and you can't imagine how the irises would look. . . ." I have a friend who slaves through the spring on extensive perennial beds at least six feet deep; whenever I compliment his work, he says wistfully, "Of course, when this was my grandmother's garden, the beds were at least twenty feet deep. . . ."

I like to take my own private garden tours of what's missing, especially in the Rhode Island village where people have been in the same beds for generations. I pedal my bicycle wistfully past the fragrant old roses that used to cascade over that ancient stone wall, or the field that used to be a riotous dazzle of wildflowers, or the corner that used to be a big bed of asparagus, so lovingly tended, year after year, by a man who eventually became so frail that one summer all I ever saw him do was sit on an old wooden stool and gaze at the feathery haze of his crop. All gone.

I miss them—blooms, beds, and gardeners past. The scars of what is gone are as evocative as what is there. I am the type of person who can (sometimes) be so focused on what's behind her that she loses sight of what could be before her. Hurtling forward, looking backward. The impossibility of the past can have a greater allure than the possibility of the future; there's a seductiveness about memory that can leave reality looking quite pale. Too much of this leads to despair.

Oh well, so what if I fell hopelessly in love with the heady sweetness of old roses or the radiant brilliance of a gnarled limb? There are others out there still to be discovered. But what a gift to have been so taken that you will always see what is no longer there.

UNPAVING

Everybody in my family gets on my case about my drive-way. Yes, it is deteriorating. Those New York winters are tough on paving. At least half of the asphalt (nasty stuff) has crumbled away under the pressure of thirty or forty years' worth of cars, milk trucks, moving vans, and all manner of vehicles carrying people who come to fix one thing and leave something else a little more broken-down. A bull-dozer was sent to do the work of a snowplow one stormy day, and left rivulets in the drive while removing a chunk of stone wall and an old tree peony. Tree roots and ice have done their work as well. The driveway has heaved itself open down the middle and exposed a vein of red brick underneath; sadly, the asphalt must have been laid over the original brickwork set down at the turn of the century, of which only the front walk survives. The driveway is in a state of utter collapse.

I like it that way.

For years now, well-intentioned construction companies have scribbled their diagnoses, along with paving estimates, on their cards, and tucked them into my kitchen door. One day while I was at work, a kind neighbor went so far as to spread some asphalt left over from the repaving of his own driveway onto the bottom of mine, in an attempt to make a presentable patch of the portion that meets the street. He meant well, but I got a nasty surprise, and didn't appreciate the gesture. It looked awful to me for a few days, and then it too got swallowed up in ruination. No Band-Aid will help; my driveway is too far gone. A friend has confided that he feels I have created a moat around my house—a comment that might bear further inspection. Someday. My parents, my sister, my children, my friends rail constantly: Don't I see how awful it looks? Don't I know what could happen to a car that pulled in too fast?

Well, that's the point, sort of. When the driveway started to get really bad, I decided to ignore it on the grounds that it was safer. My children often played at the top of the drive. A rough road forced everyone to slow down. Both boys roller-blade, and the younger is a speed demon on his skateboard.

A nice, smooth driveway would have made a great launching pad into the street. That was my story.

But now the story has changed. The swing set lies dismantled by the side of the drive, one of those skeletal remains of childhood. My skateboarder has moved on to concrete ramps and steel grind rails. The kind you find in parking lots. The only one trying to slow down around here is me.

I think the best part of my garden is in the front, unusually enough. If you drive quickly up to the house (or if you blink at just the wrong moment), you miss the view. Even walking home from the train, as I do most nights, I love having to be more careful of my footing in all those gouges and pits. I've lately noticed a beautiful new moss colony creeping across the crumbling brick. I'm forced into a kind of decompression, in a small way, upon coming home, marking a passage from one world into another as I pick my way up to the house.

So I'm not going to repave the driveway. But I'm thinking I'll lay down a drawbridge soon enough.

SHARING

A friend is about to start sharing her apartment with her boyfriend, who is moving from the West Coast to live with her. This is the same friend who, six years earlier, was buying her first home by herself. How the wheel turns. Since he is making the sacrifice of miles, I guess it is only right that she should be prepared to make the sacrifice of square feet. Their conversations about sharing her space are strained; it seems to be a trickier subject even than sex or money. It seems to surround those things. She's a nervous wreck.

She has never lived with a man, and she's in her mid-forties. I haven't lived with anyone since my marriage broke up, but I was always surprised how easy and natural it felt to live with my husband. I found romance in the ordinariness of waking up with someone, and setting the table with the same someone. In the last few years I have been so reluctant to share my life that I haven't spent a week with a lover, much less enough time to think about allocating rent. Years have gone by in loner mode and I'm beginning to wonder if I have gotten too settled in these ways, as comfortably as I had once been settled in those other ways. The closest I've come to living with anyone is to lend my country house to a friend for a couple of months after his divorce. Naturally I stayed away; he had a wonderful time, and introduced little residual mysteries in and around that house. I am still looking for the corkscrew, the big dictionary, and the small omelet pan, to say nothing of things I don't even know I've lost.

Yet, I do share my house, on a day-to-day basis, with two boys. And share is the operative word here. I feel my house is as much theirs as mine, a wonderful thing. They reciprocate: everything that is mine is theirs. This is especially true when it comes to the bathroom. Never mind that there are three in the house. Only mine will do.

I've never gone in for this two sinks, two cabinets, two-of-everything-for-him-and-her thing. There is one tub, one shower, one toilet, one sink, one armchair. One set of towels—and that just happens to be the most difficult thing to negotiate between me and the boys. One set, after all, does contain enough towels for everyone to get dry. But my sons don't seem to understand the concept of using a towel, and then hanging it to air out for the next day. How many times have I wandered into the bathroom only to discover a heap of soaked linen on the floor, puddles all around. I spent months drilling into my youngest son (the worst offender) the concept that towels need to spend time on towel bars, that that was their natural habitat, the way monkeys need to hang in trees. To no avail. We seemed to be going nowhere fast. Then an event occurred that made me realize that we weren't dealing with cotton, but with a much more complex genetic fabric.

One day Theo came down for breakfast, in his usual daze, carrying his wet towel. He is not a morning person, to put it mildly. As his older brother and I watched, dumbfounded, he walked to the trash can, opened it, and dumped in the towel. "Theo!" I cried. "What are you doing?" But I knew I had peered into the subconscious mind of a man, young and unformed though it was. I knew I was getting a glimpse of a man's inner drive, and it went something like this: Use. Toss. Use. Toss. Use. Toss. . . . My own son.

I've always felt that it was part of my lot in life, having borne two boy infants, to raise them into the kind of men whom enlightened, intellectually developed, emotionally independent, commercially successful women would like to meet. (You know, the man who will open doors, lead in the dance, make reservations, fly a plane, offer me his arm, carry my bags—unless I wanted to do all that myself—and still be a sensitive feminist.) In other words, I didn't want to be responsible for sending two more chauvinists, or two more princes, or two more big babies, into the world. This is tricky, because as a mother of course the only thing I want is for my children to remain big babies, and I want to spoil them and keep them close by so that they are utterly dependent on my ministrations. Fat chance.

But the idea of training them for their lives as men did give me a direction for talking to my youngest son, once I got him to pull the towel out of the trash.

"Theo," I said firmly, "I will not share a bathroom with a man who leaves soggy towels on the floor. That is not the kind of man I want using my towels."

This remonstrance worked so well that I realized my big mistake in son-rearing had been to treat my children as, well, children, instead of as future men. The next time we gathered for dinner, and they grunted and growled big nothings in response to my questions about what happened at school, and then fell silent, I gave them the How Are You? lecture. I told them in no uncertain terms that I would not share a table with men who didn't know how to have a conversation with a woman, men who found their own thoughts more fascinating than anyone else's. I refused, I told them, to let them become the kind of guys I sometimes met on those proverbial blind dates—I call them Juke-Box Boys. Slip in a quarter, and an hour later the show tunes are still playing. That did the trick. Even if the "How are you, Mom? What happened at work today?" is a shade sarcastic, at least the form is there. Feeling will follow form, I'm sure. At least they're young.

All of which is a long way of getting around to my friend's

anxiety about sharing her space. The first person she called, when her lover told her he was moving east, was her architect. Smart cookie. After figuring out how to partition off the colony, she feels much more secure about how she is going to negotiate the drama of the square footage. Funny how many important things get down to the simple act of storing sweaters and putting away suits.

Or hanging the towels to dry.

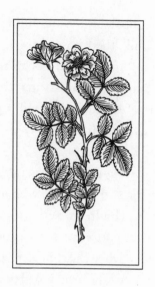

STONE WALLS

I have decided to spend some serious money on my garden, and this is a sign of good health and harmony returning to my feelings about my house. Especially because what I want to spend money on is the building of a big, beautiful stone wall.

Now, you might think that building a wall, especially a wall of the proportions I have in mind, is a bad sign. A wall might seem more symbolic of shutting things out, rather than letting things in. And to a certain extent, that's what I want to do. My neighbors' yards are sliding into mine; I live at the bottom of a hill, their houses are at the top—so, for example, when I'm on my third floor I'm at the level of their first floors. Retaining walls—now there's a pregnant phrase—were sort of haphazardly built nearly a hundred years ago, and they're slowly but surely giving up, flattened by the weight of all they hold up.

Then there is the matter of the neighbors themselves, who happen to be the sort of people who buy so much play stuff for their still tiny children that they could easily provide entertainment for an entire nursery school. I shudder to think what will arrive when the children begin to have some say in the matter of what they want to play with. The neighbors have positioned all that equipment strategically far from their house—as close to my garden as they could get without tipping over into my yard. Well, who can blame them? I wouldn't want to look at all that neon plastic and crisp cedar either, if I didn't have to. Don't get me wrong, I love the sound of children's voices squealing delightedly on the swings—well, I did when they were mine. I don't love the anxious watch for trouble, the feeling that some little soul is going to fly off and come sailing and bouncing down into my garden. And I can't help it; I worry. Once a mom, always a mom. A wall would stop the children's tumbling—and the spilling of balls and wheels into my yard, too. I get it, finally, about fences making good neighbors.

I toyed with the idea of fences, in fact, and spent lots of time looking at fences and imagining them unfurling across the back of my lot. But while I've seen plenty of admirable fences around other people's gardens, I've never wanted to take one home with me. Stone walls are another matter. I've been known to drive off the road, so spellbound am I by the sight of an ancient stone wall ribboning its way through trees and across pastures. The attraction has something to do with an impassive beauty and heft. Your eye wanders across the jigsaw of rocks and you wonder how they've been made to fit so well, who could move such heavy things with such delicacy? How could they stay together so long?

It is in the very nature of a high stone wall to give a sense of protection. Who doesn't want an embrace as strong and steadfast as that of a stone wall? Unlike a sweet picket fence, a stone wall isn't going to rot and tip over. Unlike the elegant clapboard fence, a stone wall isn't two-faced; there's no back or front to negotiate.

The impulse behind the new wall is less about keeping things out and more about keeping things in, more about a sense of enclosure. Sure, stone walls have openings: doors, passages, arches. And how about those weep holes? But I want to wrap my flanks in rocky protection. A stone wall is also a boundary, and I'm feeling a need to fortify my boundaries. Does it have something to do with finally learning to say to people—who do you think you are, talking to me that way? Does it have something to do with moving away from others' anger, hysteria, bad behavior; not being drawn into the slipstream of others' misery, no matter how much you might think you love them, or need them?

A good wall says, this is where all that is mine begins and ends. And this is how I define my property: if you are on the inside of this wall, you are inside my love, and my care, and my protection. And so am I.

BLOODY MURDER

I was awakened from a very deep sleep by screaming the likes of which I have never heard. I felt as if I were in the jungle, but I wasn't: this was the edge of New York City, after all. I lay petrified in bed as I tried to fix in my mind what were those sounds, where were they coming from? Something animal, something full of terror and rage and brutal determination. A high-pitched shrieking, yowling, snarling; a strange clicking, hammering, and stuttering. I couldn't piece it together as anything recognizable, but it was clear something terrible was happening.

Once I figured out what direction all this was coming from I got out of bed and, wrapping myself up in a shawl, went out onto the porch. The pitch of the fight had become more desperate. The magnificent dogwood at the back of the house looked as if it might shake apart with the turmoil in its limbs. There was a new moon, too faint to give off enough light to see what was happening, just enough that the blossoms—and the tree was in full, heavy bloom—were a glowing, phosphorescent white floating in the dark night. I thought I might be hearing a fight between an animal and a bird, and I ran through the inventory of sounds I had come to know in this suburban backyard. I couldn't place the clicking. Squirrel? Opossum? Crow? Owl?

I had spent the previous two days with a friend in a manic overdrive of planting, transplanting, pruning. I had finally put in the dozens of evergreens I'd been fantasizing about for years: pines, cedars, rhododendron, laurel. And without even having planned to, I overhauled the back bed, the one I see from my piano in the living room. We planted dwarf apple trees, and lilac, and broom, and stock, and peonies, and hosta. And then we carved out yet another bed, and filled it with more white azalea, and now the tide of trees that make up the front garden has cut its way across the side and back, so it seems as if my house and I fit snugly in a little cove. In an even more surprising move, I had the energy to fill several pots with petunias, which I love for their cheap gaiety, and a few more with herbs and salad stuff, and all this satisfied me enormously because there is nothing more civilized, more a sign of domestic tranquility than brimming pots.

It being early summer, all was in gorgeous, cascading

bloom and I had spent the evening surveying the yard with much the same pride I imagine a farmer would feel looking over newly sown fields. Every few hours I dragged a big sprinkler around to another corner, enjoying the cold heavy drops on my back when I wasn't fast enough to get out of the way of the fan of water. I sat, in the gloaming, admiring the deep green pools of the lawn. The heavy shade began to sparkle with fireflies. Bats whirred over the roof. It was all so beautiful that my heart filled with an extravagant new love for that house and garden. I had a sense of contentment, and containment, at being able to simply sit there and take it all in. I absentmindedly left the French doors open to the living room when I went in, and a few hours later found the darkened room magically glittering with fireflies.

So I was shocked, later that night, by the mayhem under the graceful canopy of the dogwood. I shouldn't have been; even though my lot isn't even half an acre, it contains a zoo's worth of animals, maybe because it is so thickly surrounded with trees. I'm always bumping into 'possums, raccoons, skunks, rabbits, and cats in my driveway. It is always startling: I live a minute or two from the concrete expanse of a Bronx apartment complex.

The sickening thought went through my mind that perhaps my favorite couple, the cardinals, were in trouble, that all the clicking and shrieking was about protecting a nest of eggs, or hatchlings, from someone's terrible jaws. One of my children began to cry out for me from the depths of a silky sleep, Mom, Mom, disturbed by the racket without quite awakening. I couldn't move, and I just kept thinking what should I do? How can I help? Should I throw on the lights, throw rocks, interfere with this tiny embroidery in the grand scheme of things? I did nothing. And suddenly it was all over, a few more clicks, and defeated screams, and then a dead silence. Minutes later a dark fat furry shadow stepped delicately, triumphantly, across a limb and down the tree and disappeared. No one followed.

I went inside, cupped my hand on a child's warm forehead, and went back to sleep. The next morning I walked out to the dogwood expecting to see blood dripping from the branches, or clumps of flesh or feathers and bone strewn across the ground. Nothing. Just a few white blossoms torn from the branch and scattered in the grass.

I spent the rest of the week looking for the cardinals, remembering the frightening chaos of that night's disaster and thinking how different the garden looked. Who did I think I was, to try and bring a specific order to even a suburban patch of land? But then I found myself liking the way everything looked even better. A little reminder of murderous beauty is becoming, in a garden.

DOING THE DISHES

One evening I was talking to a friend as he bustled around, clearing the table and washing the dishes after a dinner he had prepared for a rather large group. He seemed to enjoy the cleanup as much as he had the cooking— soaping each plate, glass, and pot lavishly, rinsing it thoroughly and placing it to dry on a rack. I asked him why all this seemed to give him so much pleasure. "It's my way of saying thank you to the pot," he replied, patting its bottom as tenderly as if he had just diapered a baby.

No dishwasher. No caterer. No maid. Preparation, cooking, serving—all accomplished in a spirit of steady, patient, and companionable effort. Of course, everything we build into our kitchens today goes in the opposite direction. Several dishwashers. Caterer's kitchens. Enough refrigerators to set the house humming. We need all the help we can get. Every gadget that promises a cleaner house, a better dish, is something I want in my life. I am always turning down the corners of pages in the Williams-Sonoma catalog in search of the elusive tool for better—best!—living.

It has been ever thus; our enthusiasm for the things that make housework easier isn't new. Each generation finds its own tools for liberation. And buying these things for someone else is even considered a mark of love, affection, and solidarity in the mutual assault on homemaking. ("And he bought her a dishwasher and a coffee percolator . . ." as Joni Mitchell traces the arc of a love affair.) Myself, I can't wait to buy a brand-new, superquiet, elegant dishwasher whose door won't need slamming five or six times to convince it that I'm seriously ready to get this load done.

But what have we lost in all the acquiring? Some attitude of caring for, of gratitude for, the things that make up the everyday rituals of life. One of my fondest childhood memories is of enormous Sunday meals with my grandparents in Kentucky, a place we never visited often enough, as far as I was concerned. I loved everything about it—the simple white clapboard house, the sleeping porch where I was placed in a cot so high off the ground I had to be lifted out of bed in the morning, the farm, the cows, the little pond where

I caught my first fish, my grandfather's fragrant pipe, my grandmother's radiantly sweet soul.

My grandparents served elaborate dinners after the Sunday church service, huge affairs, aunts, uncles, cousins gathered around a table piled high (in my child's eye) with chicken and mashed potatoes and greens and gravy and biscuits. And corn bread. Thick fragrant butter. Heavy sweet milk. Pecan pie and chocolate cake always followed, with ice cream. Well, at least that's how I remember those feasts. One treat after another spooling down the length of the table. Afterward, my grandparents would head into the kitchen to clean up.

Many years later, long after they had died, my father made a remark, almost offhandedly, probably during one of our incessant arguments about whose turn it was to do the dishes, about how his parents had never even owned a dishwasher, so who was I to complain? When my dad had urged them to "modernize," they refused. Cleaning up after meals was a pleasure for them. There was nothing he liked more, my grandfather explained, than standing next to my grandmother after dinner while she washed the dishes and handed them, one by one, to him to pat dry and put away. They loved each other. What more could they want? Together, they made a home.

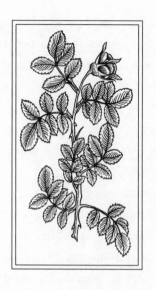

CAFÉ 222

I came home at the very end of one of those days that began with a breakfast meeting and went through dinner. I was relieved to enter my quiet, empty house (the kids weren't there); I was exhausted, and perhaps for that reason (although I am also chronically absentminded) I didn't really notice a couple of empty pizza boxes on the kitchen table that hadn't been there that morning. A few evenings later, as I was sorting the mail, I did notice lots of Chinese food containers in the trash, and thought, That's odd, I don't remember eating Chinese food, and then I promptly forgot about it. I was vaguely aware that certain foods were disappearing with alarming rapidity—things like Pop-Tarts and Tostitos and Cheerios. And then one day, I was home at lunchtime—an unusual situation—and while I was working my way through a manuscript, I heard noise from the kitchen. Voices, music, laughter. Certainly the most relaxed of burglaries; it sounded like a party.

I marched downstairs to investigate, and stumbled into the lunch party my teenaged son was throwing for four of his friends, a party that, as it happened, was a daily event. The table was strewn with soda cans, pizza boxes, and sandwich bags. Music blasted from the speakers on the sideboard. Several young men had already tucked into their meals, and I noticed (with some twisted pleasure) that my son had distributed linen napkins to his guests. One fellow was angled over the stove; appalled by the food selections at the local deli, pizza parlor, or Chinese restaurant (the three choices within walking distance), he was cooking the meal that has become a staple of the teenage boy's diet: ramen noodles. The whole scene was jolly, hospitable, lively; lunch lasted forty minutes. Everyone felt at home.

The best decorating move I ever made in my kitchen was to haul in the old leather sofa where we now eat, read, nap, and talk while someone's cooking. But the second-best move was to get rid of the adjoining family room, the room with the playpen, the block box, and the bins of toys spilled out on the floor. Once the days of babyhood were over, I packed up the plastic and put a big wooden table into that nook—

never mind that the dining room table is (redundantly) right next door. This has become a homework table, and a drawing board, and, for the last few years, it is Café 222, named for our address.

The boys' conversation, as far as I can gather (so I eavesdrop a little, wouldn't you?), ranges from comments about teachers to elaborate recitations of *Saturday Night Live* segments. It's been wonderful to follow the group's lives through the traces of what's left behind; I've watched the CD pile change from the Beatles to Bob Dylan to Ravi Shankar to Miles Davis (no Rage Against the Machine for this set; they leave all that to their younger brothers). Sixteen seems to be an age when boys shut down around their mothers; they're aware of every move you make, and they are ready to pounce with an ironic comment the moment you cross some invisible line. But they give off an air of vacancy. It's the sort of thing that makes you really appreciate their moments of presence. I'll take my teenager's company any way I can, even if it is through the medium of our kitchen as it records his comings and goings.

I have had to teach the guys some things about fine dining, to say nothing of housekeeping. We had a mouse invasion from food souvenirs left on the floor; the table sometimes develops a sticky film of spilled food—you can read it, drying there, its own exotic language: who had what for lunch (naturally I always find it the next morning when my newspaper gets glued to the table); I came home late one night to find a burner still lit, the flame dancing merrily into the air.

Still, I love Café 222. I'm pleased that my child not only has a key to the house, but that he feels free to use it—yes, without asking permission; that's the point: it is his house, too—and to share his home, his table, with his friends. Everyone knows love comes in the kitchen door.

THE EMPTY NEST

A lot of my friends are sending their children off to college, and so they are facing the proverbial empty nest for the first time. They are very upset. Understandably. Sure, every once in a while I hear from the person who feels suddenly liberated from the demands of teenagers, who feels she can reconnect with her husband, and with her own life. Reclaim that room. Redecorate. But mostly what I'm hearing is wistfulness, melancholy. She's gone. His room is silent. How could I have ever wanted peace and quiet? Awful how the refrigerator stays full so long. Incredible how my clothes don't disappear into someone else's drawers. Time to take the swing set down; it hangs so emptily. Where did the time go?

I am completely capable of sitting in a restaurant watching couples play with their babies, and melting into a reverie of longing. Where *did* the time go? How do they grow up so fast? Were mine ever so small? Did one tiny fist ever clutch at my finger so tightly?

How often do we get to rehearse for separation? My oldest son recently decided he wanted to move his bedroom up to the third floor of the house, to the room that I was using as an office. A room, I might add, I almost never entered; somehow, despite repainting and rearranging, I had never been able to transform it from my ex-husband's office to my own. I had decided that some mental blocks couldn't be tackled head on, and I simply closed the door on that one. Alex had been eyeing the real estate; he offered to trade rooms with me. "You can make my bedroom into your office, and you'll be right next to Theo's room, right down the hall from your bedroom, and it is much cozier," the pitch began. Sold.

But had I known what a project it was going to be, I wouldn't have capitulated so quickly. Packing him up was one thing, quite another was packing up a room I hadn't thought I was using, but was, a repository for every paper and picture and file I didn't want to look at, and couldn't resist poring over, now that it was time to move them. I decided on a massive cleanup.

Alex and I went through shelves of baby books; some

were easy to consign to the giveaway pile. Others we had to keep, remembering who had given the gift, the grandmother, no longer alive, who had held him in her lap and read and patiently, reassuringly reread it night after night after night, making sure the story came out okay every time. Toys mostly went, but there were plenty that I couldn't let go of, hoping that someday I would see them in my grandchildren's tiny hands. Boxes of baby snaps; naturally I'd never gotten around to putting them in albums. We lost hours over those boxes—and found years and years. I understood, suddenly, why my babies looked like little old men—all babies do, at first. God's way of showing parents their children's old age, since we won't be around to see it for ourselves.

The move took days, and was a huge success for the teenager who now had command of an entire floor of the house. Naturally Theo was put out, until I invited him to share my office space. (Not much threat of invasion there, since he's the kind of child who prefers lighting incense and listening to music over doing his homework. Like his mother before him, I might add.) It took me weeks to get used to the change. A new pattern for the bedtime ritual. Furniture creaking in a different corner of the house. And Alex's childhood room completely dismantled. Gone. I hadn't realized I would miss it as much as I do. And I was startled by how easily he let go of it.

As a divorced parent who shares custody of her children, I have been going through the emptying of my nest on a pretty regular basis for years. Every week the children leave, on to their other nest; every week they return to mine. You would think I'd be used to it. But every once in a while a huge resentment yawns up in me, and I feel how unnatural it is that I have lost half their lives, in such an untimely manner. I know how healthy and good it is that they don't feel they have lost either parent. And I know that I have used my time alone well, productively—and that the time alone has been good for me. But I also know the transfer back and forth, from one house to another, has been difficult for the boys. No matter how hard we try to remember things, no matter how much stuff we have bought in duplicate so that the boys have full rooms at either end, there's always a sense of never being completely home. And it is as true for me as it is for them. Am I nobody's full-time mom?

Is that the real upset of the empty nest? You're no longer full-time? Of course, once you are a parent, you are a parent for life, no matter what happens. It is the only point, in human love, beyond which there is no return. We are all well-versed in the platitudes of letting children fly away. Once mine have flown, there's a part of me that would not mind if they returned home forever. That's simply because I cannot quite fathom how I might have taught them the most important thing of all—how to live without me.

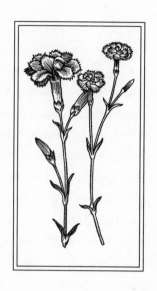

SILENT NIGHT

Once again Christmas was coming, and once again I wasn't going to put up a tree, in keeping with the tradition of the last few years. I didn't have the heart for it. It seemed a silly thing to do, all alone. For years, I left the boxes of beautiful ornaments packed away in the attic. I'll admit that every once in a while, maybe, say, in the middle of summer, when it was an utterly useless thing to do, I would open the boxes, and unwrap a couple of the tinselly, fragile, gorgeous, hopeful things. And then I would carefully pull the tissue back around the memories, and tuck them back into their nests for a few more years. I missed them, but all in all they seemed more trouble than they were worth.

Then one night my beloved friend Gary called, and wanted to know when the tree was going up. Everyone needs a friend like Gary, the kind of person who has no tolerance for wallowing self-pity in the face of something as remarkable as the holiday season. I reminded him that the tree hadn't gone up in quite a while, that the whole thing was pretty fraught. "That's ridiculous," he said. "Enough's enough. Do I have to come out there and do it myself?" That caught my attention.

Let it be said that of everyone I know who celebrates Christmas, two people close to my heart are the living embodiment of the holy day: Gary and my sister Nicole. They are people full of love and hope, faith and loyalty, renewal and celebration. Which is not to say either one isn't capable of spectacular bursts of cynicism or anger or self-indulgence. It's just that they have a nearly miraculous ability to recover, and to turn toward the bright, happy side of life. To believe that there's a star that guides us. So I pay attention to what they say.

The morning after my scolding from Gary (who, at the beginning of December, was already blasting John Prine's Christmas CD before he went off to work), I called Nicole. She was planning a Saturday run to our local tree sale; I asked her if she would pick up a tiny tree for me—something no more than two feet tall. She agreed, but when I went out to get the *Times* the next morning, I nearly fell off the porch tripping over a five-foot behemoth. "There is no such thing as a two-foot tree," Nicole said when I called to thank her, and complain, in the same breath. "They don't make them that small." Which is funny when you think about it.

I ignored the tree all day, stepping over it to go in and out as I made trips to the grocery, the dry cleaner, the bookstore. That evening, I took pity. I couldn't let the poor thing get dehydrated. I went down to the basement and found a stand, the only one of the three down there whose bolts weren't rusted beyond use. Then I put on a Bob Dylan record; it seemed appropriate enough. It took me about half an hour, and it was a real struggle, in the course of which I felt faintly ridiculous, but as Bob bemoaned eternal heartsickness, I finally got the tree centered, pinned, and watered. I clipped off the bottom branches, stuck them in a large vase to scent my bedroom, snipped open the plastic net that held everything tight to the trunk, and stepped back.

The tree was beautiful. It was a Douglas fir and its soft, pungent scent filled the room as it shed the cold of the day. It had been grown and shipped from North Carolina, and in the quiet of my kitchen (where this whole operation was taking place) I thought about North Carolina, everyone I knew from there, those beautiful mountains, why they seemed to spawn so many potters and poets, the gentle sweetness of the place. I felt pretty proud of myself, having gotten the tree into place alone. I kept remembering my father struggling, every year, with our tree; the four children gathered around to help, the squabbling about who was tilting it over; the incredible aroma coming off the branches as the tree took in the warm house air. Just as he used to do, I turned the tree around and around, looking for its best side, the side that would have gotten the most even sunbath every day, being careful not to slosh the water out of the stand. I thought about how much love my father had lavished on us, through those trees, how much of himself he wanted to share with us.

Christmas and Easter are confusing times for me. Maybe every Sunday is confusing. We were raised as Christians, in a Jewish neighborhood in Connecticut. God knows how many hours I spent wishing I were Jewish, so that I could join all my classmates in their rituals. My best friends were Jewish, my boyfriends were Jewish, my favorite teachers were Jewish. I felt like an outsider, a stranger; an odd feeling, of course, for a Christian in Connecticut, since in most of the state it was the Jews who felt like outsiders. In the towns surrounding my childhood home of Stamford, towns like New Canaan and Darien and Greenwich, Jews were so unwelcome that there were rumors of real estate kitties, money into which town officials would dip in order to outbid any Jewish family trying to buy a home there. North Stamford, in the forties and fifties, became Connecticut's Jewish ghetto. Improbably, it was there that my father decided to settle, in order to set up a small-town medical practice.

My father's family was Southern, and deeply religious; it was important to my father that we go to Sunday school every week, and that the whole family celebrate holidays together in church. When we traveled to France to visit my mother's relatives, she made a point of stopping at what seemed like every cathedral. Pushing coins through slots into large wooden boxes, she would buy long, thin, frail white candles, such as we had never seen before, and, lighting them and placing them on spikes surrounded by hundreds of other flickering candles, she would show us how to say prayers, to make wishes, to ask for beneficence and blessings. We trailed along behind her, never taking our eyes off our candles as they burned alongside hundreds of others, for fear that we would lose sight of them and be cursed. There was something mysterious about all of this, all the more so because there was something inherently exotic about my mother, raised as she had been in colonial Casablanca. So there I was, raised as a Protestant, filled with the gothic sensibilities of a Casablancan who I supposed was a Catholic, and wanting to be a Jew because my most admired friends—and those of my parents, too—were Jewish. Little wonder that a two foot tree seemed an appropriate compromise.

Little wonder, too, that the man I married was Jewish, and our children, with my heartfelt blessings, are being raised as Jews. And yet, I missed Christmas, and other holidays, and much as I tried for a while to become Jewish, I felt always that I was on the verge of being zapped by lightning for infidelity. It was, and remains, a source of confusion—and perhaps, resilience and flexibility. Luckily, my Jewish in-laws always had a Christmas tree, being assimilated Southerners, and so I really could have it both ways. Until I was on my own. Years passed, during which I made my peace with the situation by succumbing to the entropy of loss.

I tinkered with the tree and replaced the Bob Dylan with Handel's *Messiah,* a piece that, along with Bach's *Goldberg*

Variations, makes me feel in harmony with the celestial spheres. I brought a couple of boxes down from the attic. In one, coiled on top, was a rope of twinkly white lights. A bit too tasteful for the mood I was in, but they would do. Underneath lay the Garden Angel, a papier-mâché and porcelain creature whose tiny basket of vegetables spilled down her apron. On her head sat a small clay pot; pearls rimmed her wings. She flew to the top of the tree. At her feet played two musicians, wooden angels bearing lutes.

I was having a splendid time rediscovering my precious things; as I carefully peeled back layers of tissue, memories came flooding back, memories first of finding the ornaments, and of other Christmases around trees in my own house, and then, farther back, memories of Christmases in my childhood. How my father would take over the festivities, how magical his powers, as he draped glittering icicles over the tree, wound multicolored lights through the branches, placed each ornament, so precisely, nestling it into a crook of needles. Every now and then a little bathrobe would brush up against the tree, my father would gasp out a warning, too late, and a glass ball would pop off and shatter on the floor, and even that—the tiny, bright explosion, the razor-edged shards—was a thrill.

But my favorite part was late at night, long after my parents, my sisters, my brother, had gone to bed, and the house was dark and quiet, and I could sneak down to the tree, plug in the lights, and sit by myself, taking in its magnificent beauty. I would gaze into the deep color of the bulbs and let myself drift and dream.

I found myself doing exactly the same thing, decades later. Every night of that week before Christmas, I went down to my own kitchen, plugged in my small string of lights, and cast my thoughts adrift. Peace on earth. Quiet in the house. Life all around. Love everywhere. I might actually allow myself to have happy holidays. May we forever dwell in places that make us strong, ready to be surprised by joy.

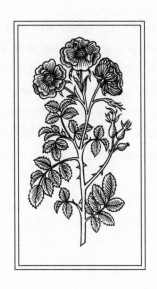

THE NEW WIFE

There wasn't much point in trying to talk about it. It was as though my teenager's heart was jammed; not so unusual at his age, but still difficult for everyone. You could see he was struggling, he just couldn't tell me what was going on. He had become withdrawn, wrapped in the kind of quiet that implies great suffering. He went about the business of school, and piano lessons, and being with friends, as usual, but it looked as though he were simply willing himself to find comfort, or at least momentum, in familiar routines.

His younger brother had been much more expressive about the new woman who, a few years after the divorce, had entered their lives. And probably he had been less troubled. Their father's girlfriend was a nice, understanding person, fairly reserved, as far as I could tell, about moving into the boys' emotional territory. I had nothing but the usual clichés to say about her. If anything, Theo, in his adorable, conniving, flirtatious way, was trying his best to take advantage of the new situation, to use it to play angles in our household, establish more privileges. I had put an end to that pretty quickly, because with him it was easy to be straightforward. When, one night, he started cajoling for another round of back rubs, neck rubs, face rubs—a ritual we had established years ago as an incentive to start the endless bedtime routine a little earlier in the evening—I refused. It was already quite late, we had been through half a bookshelf and a gallon of water. "We'll do it tomorrow night, honey," I assured him. He started whining, manipulating shamelessly. "But Dad's girlfriend gives me a massage whenever I want."

I grabbed his little pajamas by the lapels, and jerked him upright in bed, pulling his small face close to mine. I was whispering, but there was no question about my anger. "Don't you ever talk to me about another woman again, Theo." His eyes widened in amazement, I realized how crazy it all sounded, then I let him down gently, with a huge kiss and hug. He loved being talked to like a man.

And that was that.

With Alex it was a different matter.

He wasn't trying to figure out what was in it for him, with

the girlfriend. He was simply living through what it was doing to him. He was a conservative child, who depended on routine, who craved repetition, who thrived on pattern. His father and I, though no longer together, had worked hard to give him order. It was against that stable background that he felt comfortable enough to explore his own subtle eccentricities, of which there are many.

When their father announced that he was getting married, the boys were happy and excited and proud, and generously rehearsed with me their precise roles in the wedding. Under the circumstances, everything seemed peaceful and smooth. But Alex wasn't talking. The clouds would come through, settle over him for a while, and then pass.

The trouble—the big withdrawal—came during the honeymoon. I hadn't seen such gloom settle over my son since the year after his father and I had split up, and it was painful to see the return of such sadness. I guess I knew he was worrying about how he would fit into the marriage, but he couldn't tell me that. The worst of it came when he didn't show up for dinner one night, and after calling around to his friends' houses, it dawned on me to call his dad's house. Alex answered. "Time for dinner, Al. Time to come home." "I already ate." I was alarmed. "Did they come home early? Are you eating with Dad?" "No. I'm alone. I found a can of beans and I ate that." I could see him, sitting in the empty, cool house, brooding, the light in the kitchen getting dimmer and dimmer as night fell. The thought of him spooning cold food from a can, alone, like a tired, lost old man, broke my heart. I begged him to come home.

He arrived looking utterly defeated, and I folded him in a hug. I felt for my child's pain; once again I was helpless to do anything about it. "It isn't even the wedding," he said. "I just know they'll have a new baby. I'll be going from your house part time, to his house part time. The baby will be living with him all the time. I'll be nobody's full-time baby." He had the unassailable logic of a child, and was absolutely right. And of course, completely wrong.

What could I say? That full-time love had nothing to do with where you lived and how much time you spent there; that he would always be the one that made me a mother, and his dad a father, for the first time ever. That we were both as sorry as we could be for having caused him the trouble of two houses, but that we knew it was better for him in the long run than the trouble of living in one unhappy house. That I loved him with a love that should have been able to keep out any sadness in the world, and even that kind of love couldn't protect him from everything.

A few weeks passed, and then it came time for the new couple to return.

Alex decided he wanted to greet them with a gift, and he consulted his beloved Auntie Cole as to what would be good. They decided Alex would cook something and she would help. Alex's father is an ardent cook, and it moved me, all the complicated levels on which that gift was operating: that Alex would think that what his father would really appreciate was food; that Alex would be imitating the way in which his father showed love; that Alex understood the ceremonial nature of such a gift; that he would know that his father would get a kick out of having someone else cook for him.

He came home bearing an enormous apple pie, still steaming with heat. A humble offering, straight from the heart. The crust was beautifully browned, and on top of the pie Alex had placed two figures perfectly cut out of pastry—a bride and a groom, hands melted together. He had come to understand that he would "fit in" by simply, graciously granting his father acceptance of the new marriage. He had transformed misery into hopefulness and had made a remarkable peace with two households.

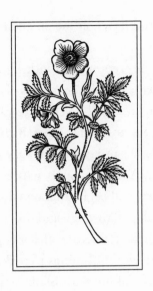

LETTING GO

Perhaps I have spent the years of recuperation cleaning closets. There's been a strange tempo in the activity, and it feels almost as if it has proceeded in symphonic movements—first movement, putting away the shards of grief; second movement, sifting for clues in the debris; third movement, building a structure in which to fit everything, as if to contain emotional chaos with scaffolding. I want my life to look well ordered, at the least. Then perhaps it will take on that quality. Somehow it has all been about holding on, though, whether I'm holding on and hiding or holding on and seeking.

Lately I've been preoccupied with figuring out what I want to take with me into the next years of my life, and what I want to let go of. I realize I don't entirely have control over deciding what goes and what stays, having attended the funerals of my mother-in-law in New Orleans and a beloved aunt in Kentucky. As I prepare my gardens for the coming winter, I know they will begin their own journey into a new year, and some will pull through and some will not. Thankfully, though, when stymied by the inexplicable, we can always turn to the world of things to make us feel as if we . have some hope of making sense of our destinies.

Back to those closets and attics and basements and boxes and trunks and drawers and shelves full of things that accumulate in our rooms. Some of my things seem no longer to want to belong to me, so I've started giving them away. The pillows that will look beautiful on N's bed, the rug that really wants to be in J's house, the dishes that ought to grace B's table—off they go. May they give my friends the same delight they once gave me. Then there are the things too heavy to carry, too full of memory: love lost in the warp and weft of that Navajo blanket, tears traced into that music played obsessively into too many nights. Be gone.

There seems to be some primitive instinct among us to load up the raft and tie down the household to get ready to pole across the river. So, what is it we want to carry with us? It's interesting to think back over the past few months and ask yourself what rooms in your house you've really used, where you've been doing your living, and what that tells you about what you need now. One friend of mine, who lives an impossibly busy life, found herself—for the first time in years—on her city terrace night after night, simply winding down in the moonlight. She never thought herself capable of relaxation, and her garden taught her that she was. The garden stays.

Same goes for things as for places: what are you drawn to, what are you buying, and what does that tell you? I find myself stocking up on books and music and wine—no mystery there—and buying photographs that, surprisingly (compared with what I used to buy), are images from the natural world. Pictures of water, and trees, and flowers, and animals. Lightning flashing across the sky, a knifepoint of illumination over a cold Maine ocean. Perhaps I'm shoring up against a growing anxiety that if we aren't more careful, we are going to lose our planet, home of homes. I'm drawn as well to pictures of ancient monuments—the Egyptian pyramids, the medieval city of Matera in Italy, the icebergs of the polar cap—as if to reassure myself that things are able to survive (in spite of us) a long, long time. In London recently I stopped at a wonderful institution of a shop, James Smith & Sons, and bought two magnificent black umbrellas, sturdy and simple, the kind you can lean on and lean under. Umbrellas to make any front hall proud, umbrellas for decades' worth of afternoon walks in the drizzly dazzle of the garden.

It is much harder to let go of big things than it is to wish for the new things that will bring happiness. Perhaps we should not need to say: let go of the people who cause constant pain; let go of the negativity that colors a room more darkly than any coat of paint. Keep close to the people you love, the ones who stay engaged and open to life, who bring joy and peace to house and garden. Take with you everything you have learned—and remain humble enough to learn more. I feel a deep need to simplify my household, but far be it from me to suggest that to do so means simply to get rid of things. Would that anything were so easy. Perhaps a new simplicity will lie in clarity about what it is we want, and what we need, from the rooms of our lives.

HONEY, I'M HOME!

Home again. You've been away awhile—a few days, a week, a month, a year or two; it doesn't matter. The lawn is unkempt, the window box spills over in a tangle of weeds, the lettuce has bolted, the swing set hangs heavily, branches are thick in the dark green shade of summer's end.

The house has been empty, shuttered, braced against intrusion. You have the key. Inside all is dim, hushed. You take a few steps forward, drop the bags, and breathe in the slumber of your rooms. The dust has settled, but somehow the air is dense with stillness. Absence has a presence. You feel it and smell it and hear it; you sense it, the way an animal senses, fleetingly, in those first few moments through the door. The rooms are as you left them. But they're not as you remember them. Absence warps, distorts. Everything seems slightly aslant somehow. Bigger. Smaller.

Perhaps you're unable to stand the silence. Or perhaps you can no longer resist the embrace of rooms poised to take you in. You're moved to break the spell. You breathe in the heavy silence one last moment and you reach for a switch. Turn on the lights. You're back.

And you begin the tender work of transforming the rooms of a house into a home again.

There is such power in the return. The return of a loved one from a trip; the return of a child from school; the return of a book; the return of a favor. The return of the swans to the pond, the return of the flowers in the bed, year after year. We experience return so often in the routine of our daily lives that we forget to notice its magic.

One of my friends was shocked when she found out that I frequently drive the three hours to my country house alone in the middle of the night. "Who knows if you've gotten there safely?" she asked. "Who do you call?"

No one. And that's been the case for such a long time, with intermittent reprieves, that I didn't even understand my friend's concern for a while. I thought it was quaint, until I remembered back to the days of being married, when someone lived at the other end of the line, and I could get someplace and call and say, I made it safely. Now, even if I do have someone in my life who might care, I've gotten so used to operating independently that it doesn't occur to me to relay the astonishing news. That's what you do only if you have left someone waiting or wondering or worrying in the place where you live together, where you expect the daily contact.

I always used to come home at the end of a day at the office, and throw open the door, and because it was comic and wonderful to be able to, I belted out "Hi, honey, I'm home!"

It sounds strange, but I still say it. Coming home is one of my favorite moments of the day, not less so because I'm greeting an empty house. (If the children are with me, even better, but they always look a little startled when I say it with such gusto. Of course you're home, they're thinking. Big deal. I'm the only one thinking, Thank God.)

When the first home you ever made was with someone else, as mine was with my husband, it can be very difficult to believe that you have the right to call what you are now making by yourself a home. We all have fairly hidebound attitudes about what constitutes home; many of us—men and women—simply dwell in waiting for our next partner, maybe even subconsciously postponing the homemaking. And that's fine. There is no right time to begin again; the spirit has to move you. Returning to a house is the easy part. Bringing a home back to life, that's trickier.

Love does not stop. Energy doesn't stand still. And neither do our homes. They're pulsing with all that we carry in; they vibrate, hum, resonate with every cry and murmur and snap and cheer of our hearts. They are our second skins, the shells we build, like snails, enlarging and encrusting with the whorls of our days, months, years. They are the most private and most telling of places. There they stand, for the world to see. And for us to make of them what we will.

Home is the place we control, the place where we have the final word about what goes where, what stays, what feels comfortable, what is life-enhancing. Home is the place into which we invite love and from which love prospers and emanates. There is always room for more. When we were kids, my father would say to each of us, I love you with all my heart. And I would protest, jealous of my siblings, But, Daddy! If you love me with all your heart, how can you give anyone else all your heart too? I understood it when I had my two sons. Our chambers swell with happiness. Our houses fill and brim.

When you think about it, much of the hustle and bustle of our daily lives comes down to making our homes. Nothing more and nothing less. When we turn our thoughts to how our houses should feel, we are doing something that our mothers and fathers did, and their parents before them. We're acting on a desire to return home. To a haven, a place to protect ourselves and the ones we love. A place for sadness and celebration, for despair and love. A place that gives us strength to go out and embrace the world. A place that is its own world.

When we make a home, we honor life and all its blessings.

So go ahead. Turn on the lights, and let it ring out.

"Honey, I'm home!"

ACKNOWLEDGMENTS

I would like to thank the friends and readers without whose guidance and faith and love I would never have seen this book through: Gary Fisketjon, Bonni Benrubi, Dennis Powers, Kathleen Bush, Jamie Kay Pfeiffer, Judy Edersheim, Judyth van Amringe, Caroline Cunningham Young, Zoe Mandes, Rachel Greenfield, Joy Hyde, Eleanor Vellis, David Carey, and Richard Fleischner. Fred Woodward, Theo's godfather, captured our children's domestic bliss over the years, and I turn to his photographs, and to him, as a touchstone for what matters. My pen pal Roger Kirby's generous and astute comments were an inspiration—and a revelation. Elizabeth Pochoda has nurtured my monthly column for *House & Garden* for five years; it is to her exacting standards that I will always try to write.

I am grateful to the editors at Scribner who took me in, Nan Graham and Sarah McGrath, and took such good care of me. And I'm grateful as well to Si Newhouse, Steve Florio, and James Truman for turning on the lights, once again, at *House & Garden*. My friend and partner at the magazine, Brenda Saget, has done much to power the place, and me as well.

It was because Byron Dobell and Amanda Urban said "write a book" that I did. It was because of my family that I was able to—my brother Philippe, a gifted writer; my sisters Michele, a gifted teacher, and Nicole, a gifted business-woman; and my sons, Alexander and Theodore, themselves gifts. And of course, thank you with all my heart to my father, who gave me love, and to my mother, who gave me music and love.

ABOUT THE AUTHOR

DOMINIQUE BROWNING has been the editor-in-chief of *House & Garden* since it was relaunched in 1995. She was previously the editor-in-chief of *Mirabella,* an assistant managing editor of *Newsweek,* executive editor of *Texas Monthly,* and a literary editor of *Esquire.* Dominique Browning lives in New York with her two teenage sons.